LIKE THE ALCHEMISTS, T[illegible] TO
HAVE THE ABILIT[illegible]
THEIR OWN P[illegible] E

UNDERSTANDING INSURANCE

How does it work?

What should you know?

What to expect for the future?

Eric Lefebvre

Understanding Insurance

For information contact

http://www.understanding-insurance.org

all.about.insurance.mechanics@gmail.com

Book and Cover design by the author with the help of Canva

ISBN: 978-3-9525102-0-9

First Edition: May 2019

To the two Cs and A but also my family and friends (a long list of people who have always provided their support)

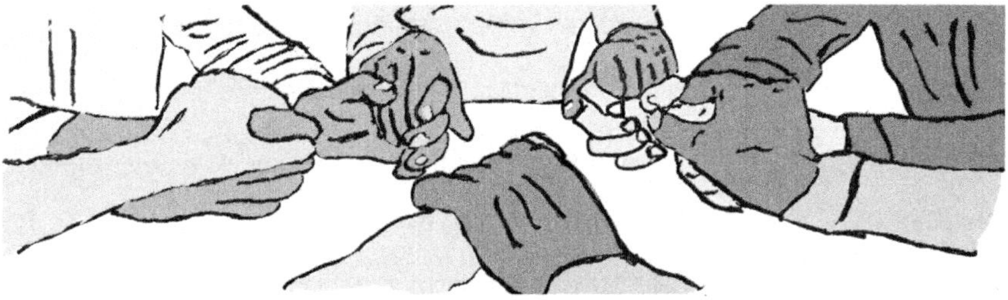

CONTENTS

If I had my way, I would write the word 'insure' upon the door of every cottage and upon the blotting book of every public man, because I am convinced, for sacrifices so small, families and estates can be protected against catastrophes which would otherwise smash them up forever.

It is the duty to arrest the ghastly waste, not merely of human happiness, but national health and strength, which follows when, through the death of the breadwinner, the frail boat in which the family are embarked, founders and the women and children and the estates are left to struggle in the dark waters of a friendless world.

Winston Churchill

Introduction

The scarcity of knowledge

"There is no greater agony than bearing an untold story inside you."
— Maya Angelou

The need to write about Insurance: **Switzerland, spring 2018**

For the past four years, consultants have come to my office with the same question: "Could you explain to us how insurance works?"

My answer would always be the same: "Sure happy to do so" and then I would stand up and start drawing flows and explaining some of the mechanics with the help of basic examples. I was able to give them the basics and tried to get their attention to what was behind the processes. Their reaction was often the same, opened eyes and surprised faces! They were encouraging me to write about this and if possible ascertain (or not) “common beliefs” regarding insurance.

Having spent more than 20 years in this industry, I have also noticed that, surprisingly, only a few people from within, understand the business model and its risks but also its financials. For instance, why do we say that the balance sheet of an insurance company is liability driven?

This book is to provide an answer to this type of question. I am providing some details about insurance and its mechanics with the help of (hopefully) simple examples. This book is not about actuarial sciences, although there will be some calculations displayed in a few chapters. The objectives are to provide the tools and some basics to anyone (customers, consultants, students or employees) who what to understand this industry.

The first chapter (**a little bit of history**) provides the origins of life and non-life insurance but also what our ancestors already discovered. We are introducing in this chapter what is at the core of insurance.

The second chapter (**the beauty of the float**) introduces what happens when a customer pays her premium and the consequences for an insurer. This chapter aims to familiarise the reader with the "insurance language" and the investment opportunities for the insurers.

As we covered the premiums in our previous chapter, the third chapter (**Reserving – a ticking time bomb challenge**) explains the possible difficulty with setting up a reserve. With a real case, we are covering how inadequate reserves can wreak havoc the solvency of an insurer). We are also explaining the concept of solvency for an insurer, the solvency being associated to safety or stability.

There cannot be a reserve without a premium. Therefore, the fourth chapter (**the enigma of insurance**) covers how we price non-life insurance products. We are using straightforward examples to illustrate the process. We are also discussing the difficulty of pricing when there is no (or a limited) history available and use Cyber insurance as a real case.

The imitation game

As we covered non-life insurance, it is time to detail life insurance. We are doing this in two chapters. The fifth chapter (**the numbers game**) brings the "protection products" and explains the business model for these products. We use a "term life insurance" as a practical example to detail the steps to get to a premium for a death cover. We are also challenging the general perception that life insurers' profits come from high lapse ratio.

The sixth chapter (**no pains, no gains**) brings some lights on the "savings products". We are using here practical examples to illustrate the sources of income for insurers and furthermore the potential future for these products. We will also detail a real case and show how some information provided to a customer could be misleading.

By this stage, the reader should have a good understanding of the insurance industry and the power of its business model. But as we discovered in 2008 with AIG, there could be significant surprises.

As per Warren Buffet, "It is good to learn from your mistakes. It is better to learn from other people's mistakes". Our focus in the following chapters (7, 8 and 9), will be about that. We will detail what happens when (i) a line of business is not properly priced, (ii) a life insurer's assets cannot match its liabilities and finally (iii) a sovereign debt crisis takes place.

The seventh chapter (**hang on and enjoy the ride**) explains based on publicly available information what happened with AIG in 2008 and what we can learn from these events. Besides, the reader will also see that the infamous Credit Default Swaps were not the only culprit for the demise of AIG.

The eighth chapter (**ignorance is bliss**) presents the consequences of a loose monetary policy for life insurers in Japan. This chapter provides some perspectives to the current low-yield environment and the impact on the life insurance industry.

The ninth chapter (**doom and gloom**) goes back to the Greek debt crisis in Europe and describes how a French insurer nearly went insolvent because of its strategy.

With the previous chapters, we know what could happen to an insurer's solvency when a strategy does not deliver as per its expectation. It is always easy to assess a performance retrospectively but what can we do to predict the future performance of an insurer. Our tenth chapter (**all is number**) provides an easy framework to assess this.

We will measure the effectiveness of an insurer's strategy against one of his peers and provide an approach to review its financial performance.

Finally, we are ending our book with a review of the current challenges that the insurance industry is facing and a possible future.

The eleventh chapter (**in search for simplicity**) comes back to the basics of insurance and what it is all about. It also elaborates about several possible outcomes for the industry.

CHAPTER 1

HISTORY IS INESCAPABLE AND CONNECTS THINGS THROUGH TIME

When did insurance start?
What did our ancestors already understand?
What can we learn from them?

BY ERIC LEFEBVRE

Chapter One

A little bit of history

"Any fool can know. The point is to understand."
— Albert Einstein

My introduction to insurance: France, winter 1996

The insurer's sales person was there to introduce us to insurance and started providing us some historical facts and frankly speaking missed the objectives. None of us in the room understood the need to talk about Edward Lloyd nor did we get a sense of what insurance was all about? Boredom was in the room.

For his defence, one needs to admit that insurance is not one of the most exciting topics. Our trainer should have provided some interesting facts to get our attention.

Today I might ask my audience which part of a celebrity is insured and then for how much, but I could also ask them who in the room play the Lottery? Moreover, if they have heard about the possibility to get a yearly payment for the rest of their lives?

Putting aside the Jennifer Lopez case, we could discuss what people were doing in China thousands of years ago to secure their cargos.

When exploring some literature, we can find lots of interesting facts about what was done in the past to help people to protect either their physical assets (goods, boats or houses) but also their savings or lives. I will try to summarise in this chapter what the insurer's sales person never told me or probably, did not even know. These facts would help anyone to understand some key insurance concepts.

First, sorry for my British friends, the Insurance business did not start in London in the 16th century with Edward Lloyd, it started way before that!

When did it all begin?

Thousands of years ago, the Chinese merchants were protecting themselves against the chance of a ruinous disaster in the Yangtze River by dividing their goods across several vessels to spread out the loss if one sank. Each boat carried a mix of cargo from several merchants. A single loss of a ship meant a small burden for all rather than a ruinous outcome for one. They most likely did not know the concept of insurance at that time, but they clearly understood the idea of sharing the risks.

Risk pooling (or sharing) is a cornerstone of the business of insurance. If the risks can be divided among many members of a group, then the misfortunes (losses) of one could be made bearable to all. We would call this a mutualisation of risks which lowers the overall potential for significant financial loss to any one person (See the illustration 1 below)

Illustration 1: Pooling of risk among four merchants

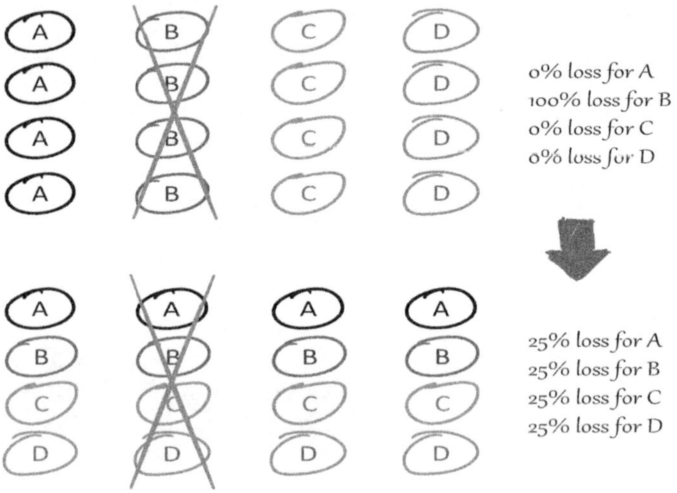

When did we see the first insurance regulation?

In Babylon around 1790 BC, King Hammurabi enacted a compendium of 282 laws that set standards of conduct and justice for his empire in ancient Mesopotamia. In the middle of rules such as "If a man knocks out the teeth of his equal, his teeth shall be knocked out", we can find a code addressing "insurance issues".

Rule 22 dealt with the robber – "If anyone is committing a robbery and is caught, then he shall be put to death", Rule 23 provided a form of 'state' compensation for the victim which is a mutualisation of the risk of robbery: "If the robber is not caught, then shall he who was robbed claim under oath the amount of his loss; then shall the community … compensate him for the goods stolen."

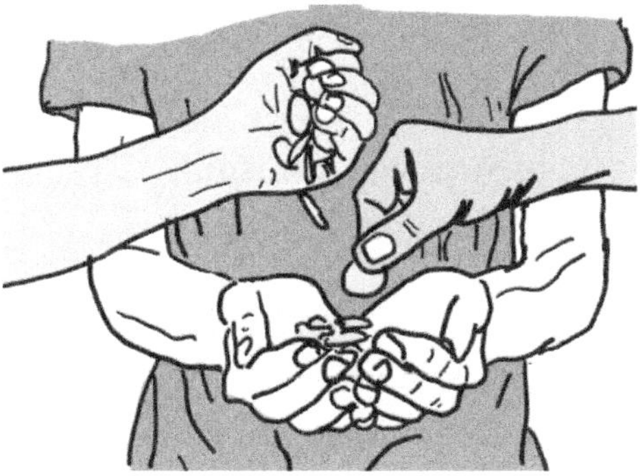

They were also at the origin of Marine insurance when enacting the concept of “bottomry”. Merchants could finance their shipping through loans from lenders. Upon the safe arrival of the goods, merchants were required to pay back the loan (also called principal), with interest.

However, if during the trip the merchandise was lost, the merchant was not required to pay back the lenders.

In a “bottomry” agreement, which is a risk transfer, the interest on the loan is the equivalent of an “insurance risk premium”: the higher the risk of loss, the higher the interest rate.

The financial consequences of an existing risk could be transferred (covered) for an amount (premium) to a third party. Today this would be called a risk transfer, the purchase of an insurance cover effectively a risk of loss from the policyholder (the client) to the insurer.

Bottomry was also practised by the Hindus in 600 BCE and was well understood in ancient Greece as early as the 4th century BCE.
The Romans went further in terms of guarantees for the shipment of goods. Titus Livy (64 or 59 BCE -12 or 17 CE) said in his letters that the contractors who undertook to transport provisions and military supplies to the troops in Spain stipulated that the government should assume all risk of loss due to risks of the sea or capture (piracy).

At the height of Roman power in the mid-2nd century AD, the Empire had around 65 million people. Rome itself had a population of 1 million inhabitants including 500,000 slaves.

With such size, Rome could not survive without getting grains and food products by road but more importantly by sea. Grain was shipped to Rome from Sardinia, Sicily, Africa, and Egypt. Oil was exported from Spain and Africa.

To fund these ventures, the Romans put in place a very complex financial system which provided loans and a form of insurance.

In other words, the Romans were encouraging people to take risks to ship goods or import goods by guaranteeing the payment of the bill in the case of an accident. Today, we can see similar set-up with the Export Credit Agencies which encourage their industry to export goods to foreign countries with the help of Trade Credit insurance.

These loans were so conventional that the Romans developed standard contracts used for each voyage.

Over time, a distinction took place between the ship and the merchandise. The ships were financed and covered under a bottomry agreement while the cargo was financed and covered under a respondentia agreement.

Illustration 2: Bottomry agreement to finance and cover shipping risks

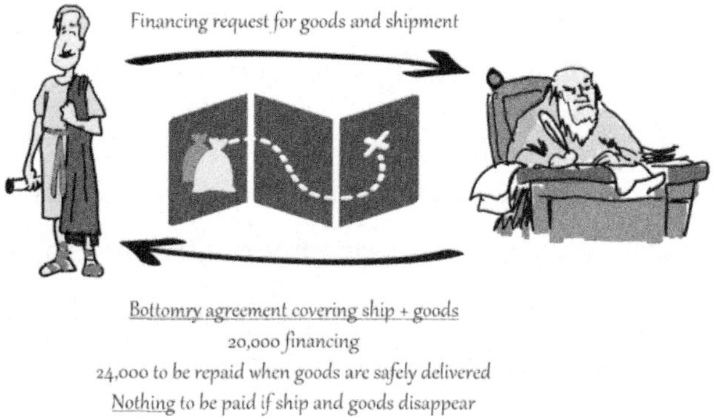

The risk of loss was with the lender; therefore, it was charging a high-interest rate to cover the risk of losing the property (vessels or merchandises). The interest rate and the principal (the borrowed amount) were payable only if the boat and the merchandise arrived safely. The price to cover the risk of loss was paid after the event to be covered. Today, this amount is charged before shipping the goods, and we call this a "marine insurance" premium. If the boat is financed with a mortgage and the hull used as collateral, the marine insurance pays the lender in the case of a loss.

When did we see the issuance of an insurance contract?

After the collapse of the Roman Empire, limited trades took place in Europe, and it took several centuries before regular overseas commerce resumed. The 11th century marked a significant shift in Europe with the Northmen (Vikings) who settled down and the rise of Italian Port Cities, Pisa, Genoa or Venetia.

The Venetians and Genoese rapidly became the merchants of the Western world, and a dramatic increase of trades took place across the Mediterranean Sea. These Italians cities dominated the shipment of goods from the east to the west. By the end of the 13th century, the Venetians also sailed out past Gibraltar up to London and Bruges where they exchanged luxury goods from the East for products of the North. The use of Bottomry and Respondentia helped the merchants to finance their ventures and furthermore cover their risks.

Illustration 3: Bottomry and respondentia

Bottomry – covering the ship

Respondentia – covering the merchandise

At the beginning of the 14th century, having "insurance cover" for a ship and merchandise was an ordinary commercial transaction. It was only a question of time before the insurance cover was separated from the loan in a bottomry.

In the Genoa archives, historians found a contract dated 1343 which provides evidence of the separation for an insurance feature (transfer or risk against a premium) from a marine loan. Genoa became the centre of the insurance business, with insurance brokers putting in place such contracts.

In addition to defining a standard insurance contract, the Genoese also gave some insurance guidelines: The insured must be the owner or at least have some interest in the covered property.

When the sum to be insured was high, the Genoese made it possible for several persons to join the contract. They were adding their names to the contract with their proportion of the sum insured. Today, we call this a coinsurance arrangement (See illustration 4 below).

Illustration 4: four coinsurers to cover a ship

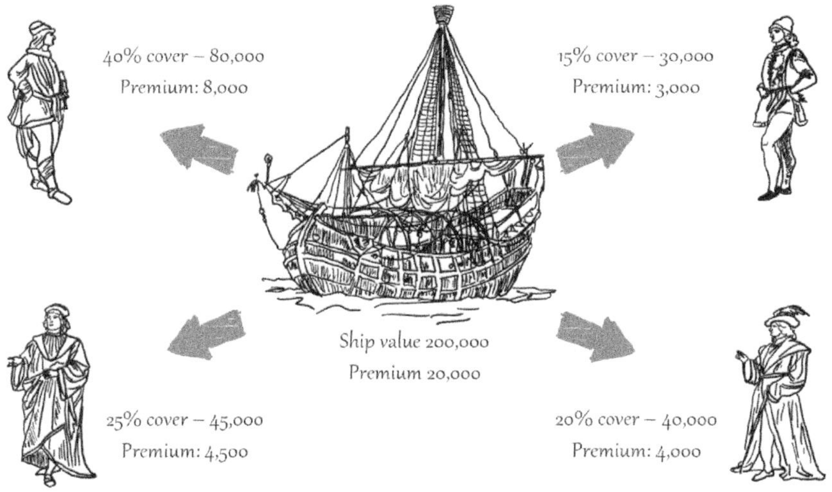

By covering in a separate contract, the risk of loss of goods against a premium, the Genoese put in place the first insurance policy. They also came up with the concept of coinsurance, which provides partial coverage along with other players.

Today we define insurance as a contract by which one party, in consideration of a premium, undertakes to indemnify another party against a specified event. Insurance firms are also acting as coinsurers for very large amount to be covered.

Over the following centuries, different types of marine insurance business took place in Europe (e.g. Barcelona, Bruges, and London). In the 16th century, the Lombards (immigrants living on Lombard street) brought to the UK the word "polizza"- i.e. a promise which is the root of the term "policy", but also the know-how for pricing and managing insurance covers.

Illustration 5: Broker General Advertiser April 22, 1746 – Lombard Street

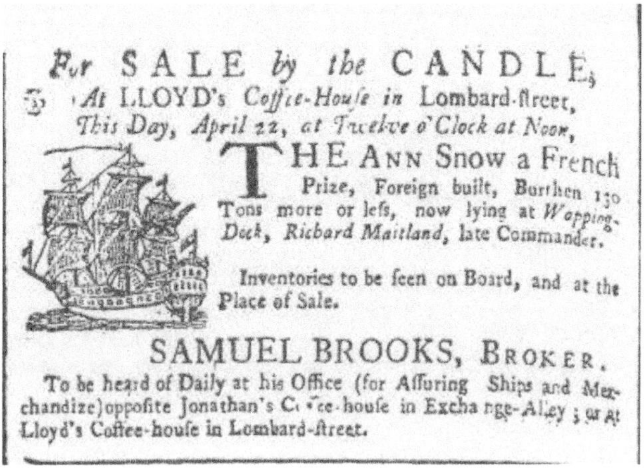

For SALE by the CANDLE,
At LLOYD's Coffee-Houſe in Lombard-ſtreet,
This Day, April 22, at Twelve o'Clock at Noon,

THE ANN Snow a French Prize, Foreign built, Burthen 130 Tons more or leſs, now lying at Wapping-Dock, Richard Maitland, late Commander.

Inventories to be ſeen on Board, and at the Place of Sale.

SAMUEL BROOKS, BROKER.

To be heard of Daily at his Office (for Aſſuring Ships and Merchandize) oppoſite Jonathan's C[illegible]ee-houſe in Exchange-Alley; or At Lloyd's Coffee-houſe in Lombard-ſtreet.

The growth of England's foreign trade in the latter part of the sixteenth century and the use of insurance to cover the marine risks increased the need for this industry to be regulated but also to accurately record the insurance policies. In 1575, the Office of Assurances was established in the Royal Exchange to coordinate and control the writing of insurance. A copy of every policy had to be copied into the policy register held at the Office.

Illustration 6: Extract of an English marine insurance policy of 1580 held in the library of the Institute of Actuaries in the UK.

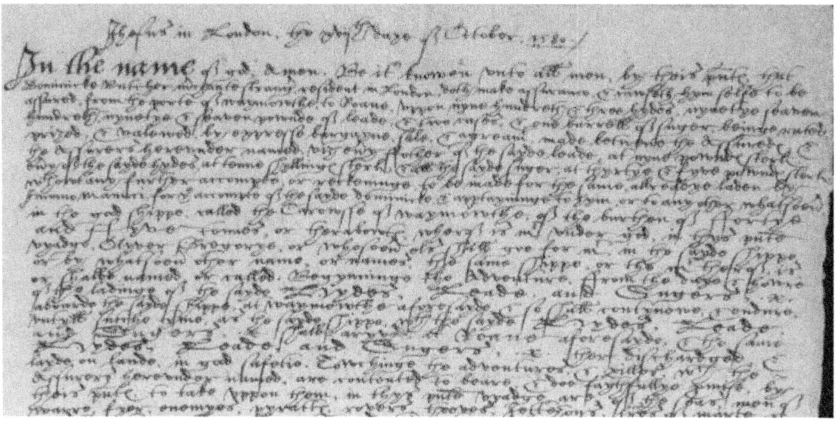

The policy starts with the following:

"Jesus in London the 17th day of October 1580. In the name of God, Amen. Be it known unto all men, by these presents, that Dominick Butcher, merchant stranger resident in London, doth make assurance and causeth himself to be assured, from the port of Weymouth to Roane, upon nine hundred and three hides, 9797 pounds of lead, ..."

Marine Insurance started in Babylon thousands of years ago with bottomry arrangements. People already understood the concept of risk mutualisation (risk sharing) and risk transfer to a third party against a premium. This practice was improved over the following centuries and finally the Genoese in the 14th century AD put in place the first marine insurance contract.

In the UK, they also understood the need to record insurance policies in a registry to avoid future disputes between the insured and insurers (this is still the case today, in most countries, insurers must maintain a policy record for each insurance contract or policy for several years after the cover ended).

People understood that they would gain financial stability by transferring and pooling their risks. This encouraged more people to create wealth and undertake risky projects that they would not have considered.

These were the seeds for the modern insurance industry as we know it today.

We know today that an increase in individuals' wealth leads to a demand for wealth protection and investment products.

With the rapid development of European trade and prosperity in the 13th century, cities in Italy and the Netherlands witnessed the creation of extraordinary wealth. Merchants were risking their money trading with others and used marine insurance to mitigate their most significant risk but what about their wealth?

As with property insurance, did we see similar trends thousands of years ago with the first creation of wealth under the Romans or the Greeks?

There are lots of interesting facts relating the very early life insurance industry which could be found in Edwin Kopf's book, "the early history of the annuity", published in 1929 and The Story of

Life Insurance by Burton J. Hendrick published in 1906. These two books are helping us to summarise what happened a long time ago.

When did we see the first life insurance cover?

In Greece around 300BC, there were religious societies known as Eranoi and Thiasoi which were covering the expenses of their members' burials.

Similar societies, called Collegia, existed in Rome, where their establishment was attributed to Numa Pompilius (753 BC – 673 BC).

The members of these mutual benefit societies paid an initiation fee and periodic contributions. The accumulated funds were used to help members of the group stricken by illness or accident, to pay for members' funerals and support their surviving dependents in death cases.

A group of people exposed to similar risk came together and made contributions towards the formation of a pool of funds. The accumulated reserve was providing financial protection against losses that may incur in the case of death, illness, or accident.

The lanuvium collegia's entry fee was at 100 sestertii plus an amphora of wine. The new member committed himself to pay monthly dues of one-third sestertius. If the member kept up with his monthly dues, when he died, the association would pay for his funeral expenses up to 300 sestertii (roughly three months' wages).

Illustration 7: Collegia fund accumulation

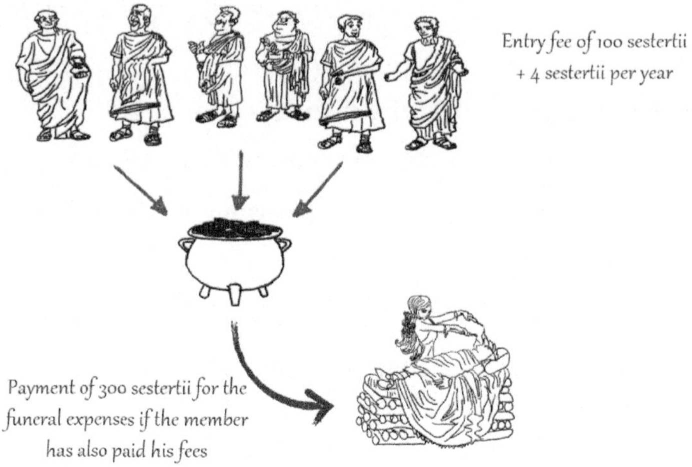

The collegia had to get additional funding to serve their future liabilities; they were most likely also relying on the members who stop paying their fees (policy lapsing).

For instance, if a person started paying at 20 years old and died at 60, the collegia collected 180 sestertii (100 + 4 x 20) which was not enough. The collegia had to find a way to cover the gap.

We have found evidence of collegia that were investing their funds to sustain their expenses.

In one inscription from the reign of Antoninus Pius (86 AD – 161 AD), the donor gave 50,000 sestertii in coins to the Collegium of Aesculapius and Hygeia near Rome with instructions to the 60 members of the association to loan out the funds and use the returns to fund their feasts and other activities.

Illustration 8: Collegia fund accumulation

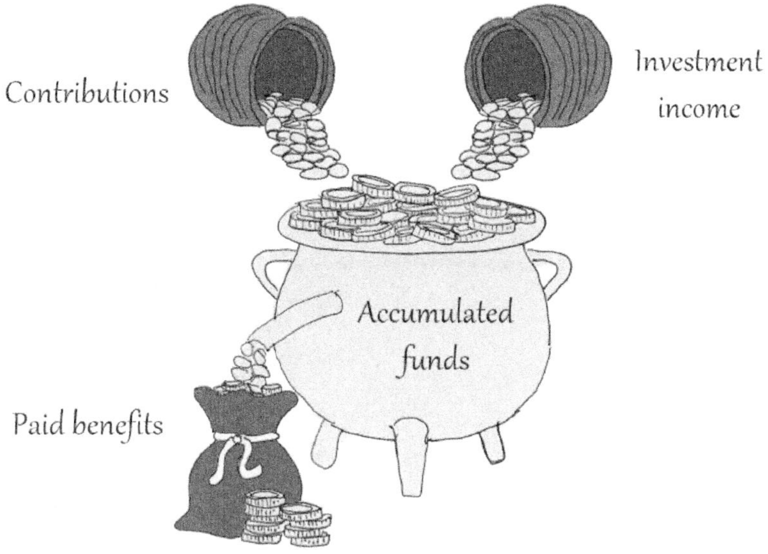

Through moneylending and real estate investments, the collegia could increase their pool of funds for covering their future obligations (liabilities). Insurers are doing something similar today.

They collect premiums and place them into an investment pool.

They use the premiums collected to fund investments, generally in guaranteed or low-risk securities due to regulatory restrictions.

When a claim is made, the money is taken from that pool and put into a cash account to pay the claim.

When were the first annuities put in place?

We define an annuity as a fixed sum of money paid to someone each year, typically for the rest of their lives.

Illustration 9: Annuity payment

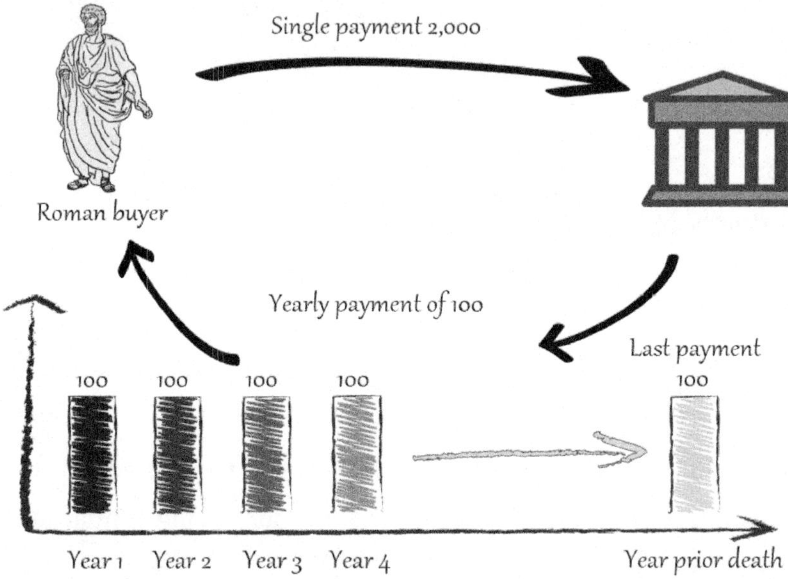

There is plenty of evidence in the "Response of Ulpianus", in the Digests of Justinian and in the Basilikon of Basil that the Romans were continually buying or selling annuities (referred as "annuum"), both for life and fixed terms. In return for a lump sum payment, these arrangements promised to pay the buyers or their designated beneficiaries a fixed yearly income for life, or sometimes for a specified period.

In the Lex Falcid (40 BC) there were provisions that the heir or heirs of an estate should receive not less than one-fourth of the total property left by a deceased person. When a dead person had left a life annuity to one or more beneficiaries, the main challenge was to capitalize the annuities. To resolve this issue, the Romans used a life expectancy table known as the Ulpian's Table.

The Roman Domitius Ulpianus (170AD – 223AD) created the very first actuarial life table ("Ulpian's table"). In this table, the "life expectancy" either represented a median life expectancy (i.e., the number of years elapsed before half the selected population is dead) or a discounted.

Table 1: "life expectancy" as per Domitius Ulpianus

Annuitant's present age (x)	**life expectancy**
0–19	30
20–24	28
25–29	25
30–34	22
35–39	20
40–49	(60-x-1) *
50–54	9
55–59	7
60–	5

**For 45 years old, the expectancy would be 60 – 45 -1 = 14 years*

The Ulpian table was the official annuity table of the Tuscan Government in Northern Italy until early in the nineteenth century.

Life expectancy tables are used to determine the present value of an annuity payment. Arithmetic and statistical material were required to come up with the adequate discount rate. Today, the cost of a life insurance cover depends mostly on the probable length of one's remaining life. Insurance firms use a mortality table which provides the rate of death among a defined population (see chapter five).

After the fall of Rome (fourth century AD), the money economy which the Romans had set up almost disappeared, and the then known world became a "goods economy". However, this did not stop the business of issuing annuities.

How did Life Annuities evolve after the fall of the Roman Empire throughout the middle age?

During the eighth century, monasteries and other religious organisations gave land in return for payments of money. The Council of Celchyth in 816 AD laid down a rule that the lands of the Church should not be charged for more than the term of a single life.

Illustration 10: Usage of land in return for payment

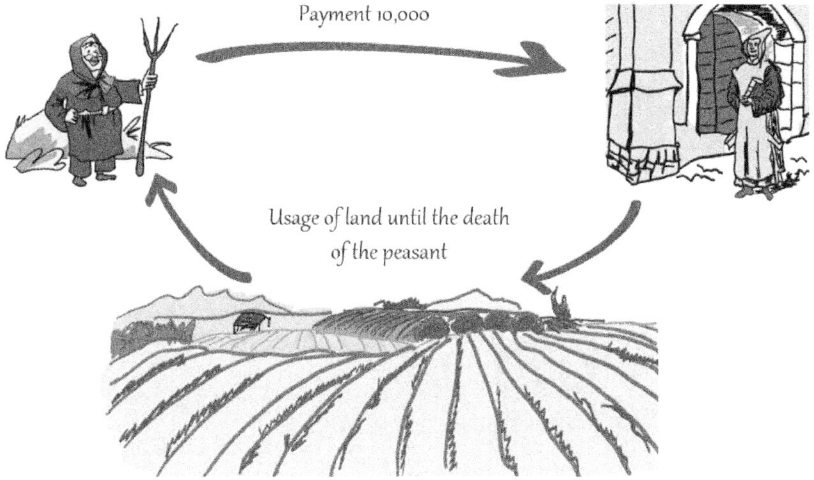

At that time and throughout the middle age, the life annuities were used to raise capital and were a form of debt owed by the towns or states. The annuity was payable for the duration of the beneficiary's life (or beneficiaries' life).

It is also worth mentioning that in the case of death, the payments to "heirs" could also take place.

In 1308, the Abbot of St. Denis arranged with the Archbishop of Cologne to pay a life annuity of 400 livres to the Archbishop in consideration of 2,400 livres paid to the Monastery. In the event of death during the first two years of the term of the annuity, 1,000 livres were to be repaid to the heirs of the Archbishop.

Illustration 11: Annuity with death benefits

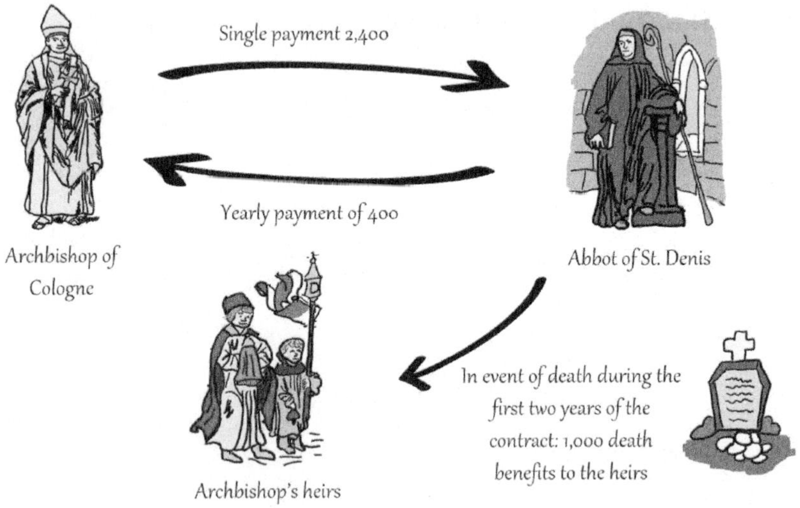

In the archives of Flemish municipalities (e.g. Tournai), we can find evidence of Annuity arrangements which were dated back to 1229 AD. For instance, in Bruges, Robert Norman and his son Baudoin arranged for a survivor annuity of 400 Parisian livres in February 1265. They provided that if the purchasing power of the Parisian livres declined, the payments were to be made in the sous of Tournai at the ratio of 50 Tournaise sous to 48 Parisian livres.

Illustration 12: Cost of living adjustments to an annuity

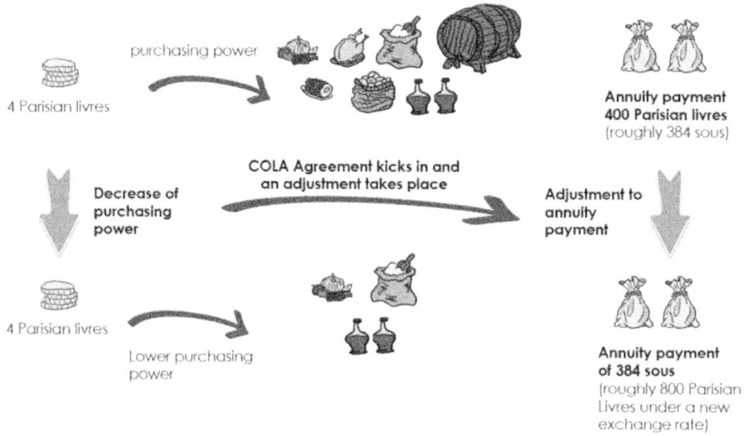

In an annuity contract, a distinction could take place between the money income and the real income (e.g. the future money's purchasing power). Today, insurers are offering to their customers the possibility to add Cost of Living Adjustments ("COLAs") to an income annuity contract. The COLA could either be a level increase (e.g. a constant 3% adjustment) or a Consumer Price Index ('CPI') adjustment. The CPI is updated January 1st of each year, and the annuity income can either increase or decrease for that year based on the change in the CPI index.

We can find "mentions" of annuity arrangements in the archives of municipalities and "policies" to identify frauds.

In Leyden (Netherlands), an annuity certificate on file for the year 1402 contains a death certificate signed by a physician. Measures were taken to encourage the prompt reporting of deaths of annuitants. In the middle of the sixteenth century, people who reported deaths of annuitants or frauds, were rewarded.

A manuscript for 1449 showed that half-yearly payments were made in June and at Christmas. An official of the town would search out persons entitled to annuity payments, post a notice on the church door, set up an office and then tell the annuitants to call for their money.

Illustration 13: Fraud avoidance – face to face payments of an Annuity

The identification of deceased annuitants was a challenge for the borrowers thus the need to rely on their declaration and to reach out to the beneficiaries by available means.

Today, insurance companies are relying on their mortality table for flagging policies and depending on the countries, they also have access to specific social security databases which help them to identify if a client died. When someone dies, it is often the responsibility of the beneficiaries to claim the money in a policy. Insurers are not required to seek out the beneficiaries.

What are the other forms of annuities issued to finance cities and states?

In the 15th century in addition to life annuities, European States and municipalities issued **perpetual annuities** to finance their wars or operations. We can find numerous information on these arrangements in France or German. In France, in 1522, perpetual annuities called "rentes" were floated at 8.5%. The collected tax on wine secured the annuities. In Germany, around 1530, the city of Nuremberg borrowed on perpetual annuities at 5%.

A perpetual annuity was a contract put in place between a borrower and a lender: The borrower promised to pay a fixed amount every year forever to a lender. The borrower's only obligation was to pay the specified amount; he could, however, at his option, choose to end the contract by repaying the purchase price (the amount which was initially borrowed). We would see this today as a perpetual bond with a call option. The perpetual annuities were secured by a revenue stream such as collected tax.

At the Renaissance and after, annuities were used as fundraising vehicles for European states and towns and were popular. The governments were using these schemes for financing their war efforts and projects.

In 1721, the French state was not able to fulfil its obligation with a total debt of roughly 2bn livres, and a Restructuring took place. Out of the 2bn, approximately 50% were perpetual annuities.

The states and towns were financing their projects and wars with the issuance of annuities (a form of debt) directly to individuals. Today, governments are issuing bonds to finance their budget deficits and are not issuing annuities anymore. They are also issuing project bonds to finance infrastructure-related projects.

The buyers of these bonds are mainly, pension funds, insurers, mutual funds, foreign (and domestic) central banks, investment banks. Due to regulations, individuals' insurance premiums or savings plans (including pension funds) are partly invested in these bonds.

In the 17th century, people could buy another form of annuities. Lorenzo Tonti, a Neapolitan banker proposed a new scheme to Cardinal Mazarin to resuscitate the French finances.

The proposed investment plan, "a **tontine**" combined the features of a group annuity and a lottery. Each subscriber was to pay an agreed sum into the pool and after that to receive an annuity. As members died, their shares were split among the other participants, and so the value of each annuity increased. On the death of the last member, the scheme was wound up.

By an edict dated Dec 2, 1689, King Louis the XIV created a "tontine royale" and raised 1,400,000 livres on his first Tontine plan. The tontine invited subscriptions, at 300 livres each, to a general fund. The French Kingdom agreed to pay the total interest on this fund to all surviving subscribers. Each member's share of the income was to cease at death and revert to those who still lived. Each member's revenue increased in proportion to the deaths of their associates in the scheme.

This scheme was the equivalent of a state loan upon which, interests were paid to the subscribers and which was entirely liquidated when the final survivor died, the interests to be paid were increasing over the years.

The Tontine met all its obligations (even after the 1721 debt restructuring) and continued until 1726 when the last survivor, Charlotte Bonnemay (widow of Louis Barbier) died in her ninety-sixth year. At that time, she drew an annual income of 73,500 livres, in return for an initial subscription of 300 livres.

Illustration 14: Tontine scheme

****

How does a tontine work?

Let's assume a tontine put in place in 1710 with 100 people paying $10,000 each – for a total of $1,000,000 and a yearly 7% pay-out – which means a $70,000 dividend every year.

As long as the 100 people are alive, each would receive a 1/100th share of the total dividend – meaning $70,000 / 100 = $700 – which is a 7% pay-out of their $10,000 initial investment.

However, if after 20 years only 50 people are alive, the $70,000 annual pay-out would be split amongst these 50 people, which means a dividend payment of $70,000 / 50 = $1,400 per person.

As more people pass away, the tontine payments to the survivors continue to grow with the final few participants receiving substantial dividend payments in their final years e.g. $70,000 for the last survivor (pretty much what Charlotte Bonnemay received from the French state)

****

In 1670 the Dutch city of Kampen floated a tontine of 100,000 florins in 400 certificates of 250 florins each. Jacob Van Dael set up the tontine and published prospectus with a prospective survival table of the 400 annuitants (see table 2).

Table 2: Van Dael survivorship table

Years	# of survivors
1	400
12	200
24	100
36	50
48	25
60*	12
64	8
68	5
72	3
76	1
80	0

**From the 60th year on the decrement is one death for each year of experience in the original table.*

Van Dael suggested that no interest be paid to pool members until 24 years had elapsed; then 15 percent was to be paid. After 36 years, 32 percent; after 73 years, 400 percent, and after 80 years 1,600 percent was to be distributed to the survivors of the original 400 (See table 3).

Table 3 Interests to be paid in the Kampen Tontine

Years	%
From 0 to 23	0
From 24 to 35	15%
From 36 to 72	32%
After 73 to 79	400%
After 80	1,600%

If we follow the assumptions of the tontine and compute the annuities per year, we will see that the tontine would have run out of cash after 74 years if the initially collected pool was not invested (see table 4 for pay-out estimates per period)

Table 4: Projection of the Van Dael scheme under the assumption that the pool of cash is not invested

Years	Pool Available at the end of the period (Florins)	Total Cash Paid out per period
From 0 to 23	100,000	0
From 24 to 35	66,175	33,825
From 36 to 72	3,935	62,240
After 73 to 79	-7,065	11,000
After 80		0

If the collected cash were invested at 5% per year without being used for covering any expenses, the town would have had more than 300,000 florins in hand, at the end of the first period, which was more than enough for covering its obligations the following years.

At the end of the 17th century, the issuers of annuities started moving from offerings which were based on experiments and trials to a more systemic approach based on mathematics (e.g. understanding of compound interest, probabilities, and mortality tables drawn from the experience of populations, ...)

The 17th and 18th centuries were a transition period to "modern life insurance" based on actuarial calculations and tools.

We are now using "period life tables" for life insurance. These tables are built with the mortality experience of a population during a short period.

With wealth creation, people were looking at opportunities to protect and grow their savings. Over the past, apart from the Romans, there has not been that much pure life insurance protection (the payment of a sum of money at the death of the insured).

There could be several reasons for this, one being that they did not have the statistical knowledge nor accurate mortality tables to price the risk of death accurately (they were missing the probable duration of the insured's life).

Life insurance as we know it today, started in the 19th century, with the possibility for people to get their risk of death covered against the payment of premiums during their lives.

To come back to my introduction to insurance, I am finding it fascinating that thousands of years ago, people already understood the benefits of pooling together their money for the good of the community. Our ancestors already recognised the need to have a pot of cash big enough to cover the risk of death and furthermore the benefits of having sound investments. The "tontines" are still in use today in Africa, and Marine insurance is still relying on some of the rules set by the Venetians.

Throughout the rest of this book, we will cover some of the concepts introduced in this first chapter but with a "modern" view. We will start first with what happens when a customer pays an insurance premium to an insurer and the positive consequences of this payment!

CHAPTER 2

WHATEVER FLOATS YOUR INSURANCE

What is the difference between life and damage insurance?
Why insurers are able to keep their promises?
What are the insurers' provisions?

BY ERIC LEFEBVRE

Chapter Two

The beauty of the insurance float

"Risk comes from not knowing what you're doing."
— Warren Buffet

My introduction to the float: **France, spring 1999**

Following a hostile Merger, I end up discussing the opportunity to join the Risk Engineering team of a global insurer. While exchanging with my future manager, we cover the latest results of the acquirer (her firm) which I did not find impressive from a technical insurance standpoint (our firm was doing better). She looked at me and said, "probably but this is not very important since our investment management arm brought lots of profits to the firm; thus, our excellent results". She had a point, not sure that she understood insurance but the analysis was spot on. This led me to start reviewing the balance sheet and income statements of insurers to understand their sources of revenues and furthermore crucial performance indicators.

However, instead of putting the cart before the horse and go straight into the business model of an insurer, it is worth understanding what happens to a premium paid for damage insurance and life insurance (also called death cover).

How do we define Damage insurance (also called General Insurance or Non-life insurance) and what are the differences with Life insurance?

General Insurances help people to protect their possessions, such as their homes, cars but also factories and other physical goods, e.g. cargoes but also non-physical risks, e.g. business interruption. These insurance contracts are "indemnity contracts" which means that if a loss (accident) does not occur, the insurers do not have to pay anything. The promise to pay only applies when a covered accident occurs, the liability materialises only when a loss takes place.

Life Insurance is a promise to pay at the death of the insured a fixed amount of money (or an annuity) to a designated beneficiary (or several beneficiaries) in exchange for the payment of a single or regular premium.

There are two types of life insurance contracts: (i) those which are pure protection policies (e.g. payment of a benefit in the event of death) and (ii) savings policies (e.g. the growth of capital with regular or singular premium invested in specific asset classes).

In the case of life insurance contracts, there is a certainty that the insurer will have to pay an agreed amount to the beneficiaries, the only unknown is when (although the mortality tables provide some indications). Since the insurer has undertaken an obligation, there is a liability even if there will not be any payment of a death benefit for 30 or 40 years in the future.

Against the payment of a premium, Life insurance and General insurance products are both covering a risk but, putting aside the type of risk covered, there are significant differences between these two fields of insurance.

For life insurance, there could be a very long period between the collection of premiums and the payment of claims, and there is a certainty that a claim will be paid and its amount.

For general insurance, the period between the collection of premiums and the payment of claims could be very short. There is an uncertainty on the volume of claims and the amounts to be paid. There is also the possibility that there won't be any claims to be paid.

How do Insurers not get bankrupt with their promises? Why are they different than Ponzi Schemes?

Insurers are not different from other businesses, at any time they must be able to meet all their obligations vis-à-vis their clients (the insured), their employees, their supplier. Without a sound cash flow planning, the insurers could be without enough money to fulfil their obligations (See example 1 below to illustrate this better).

****

Example 1: Amy and InsuR

Let's consider a person, Amy who bought last month from InsuR, a property insurance to cover her house and its content against the risks of fire, theft and some weather damage. She paid a $1,200 premium for a one-year cover and signed all the necessary documents.

Today, Amy declares to her insurer, a fire which damaged half of her property for a total loss of $120,000.
If Amy were the unique client of InsuR, she would most likely be in trouble as the insurer would not be able to fulfil its obligations and cover the claim.

However, if we assume that over the past year, InsuR managed to sell the same type of products to over 1,000 clients for an average premium of $1,200 and that Amy is the first client to declare a claim, InsuR would not have any problem to fulfil their obligations.

Illustration 15: Pool of premiums to pay claims to policyholders

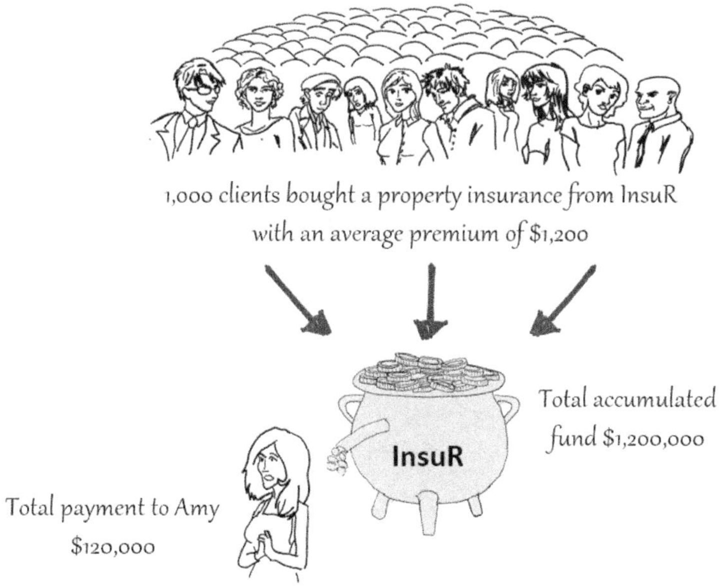

****

The more people buy an insurance cover from InsuR, the more their risks are shared, and the higher the chances that what InsuR pays out as compensation is lower than the money collected as premium.

By being able to pool together the risk of many customers, the insurers can increase their likelihood to fulfil their obligations and compensate their clients when they have a covered loss.

Insurers are not "gambling", it was probably the case in the early days of insurance described in the first chapter of this book, but not anymore. The premium charged by an insurance company is based on (i) the probability of an accident happening (which provides what would be paid in the future), (ii) the costs of running the company and (iii) the margin charged for the service provided.

Insurers could still be running a loss if they follow an aggressive commercial strategy and underprice their products or misprice their products.

We could also have Insurers who do not put aside any cash for future claims, in this case, these "Ponzi insurers" would be insurers which use the newly collected premiums for paying the past claims. However, the regulators would not let this happen.

By law, insurers must set up balance sheet reserves for ensuring that they can pay any claims, losses or benefits promised to their customers.

It is worth noticing that depending on the country when starting an insurance company; the capital requirements would be in the range of 5 to 10 million $ (before even issuing any insurance policies).

One of the critical activities for insurers is to form provisions to cover their contractual obligations. For general insurance, the most significant items on the liability side of their balance sheet are what we call the technical provisions.

Non-life insurance companies must form four types of provisions:

a) provisions for claims reported but not yet settled;
b) provisions for claims incurred but not reported (IBNR)
c) security and equalisation reserves
d) unearned premium reserves (UPR)

The items (a) and (b) are rather self-explanatory with IBNR being an estimate, since the insurer cannot know how many of the losses have occurred, nor their severity.

With this uncertainty, the insurers need to set "equalisation reserves" to protect their solvency. The equalisation reserve is an additional "buffer" to cover unexpected losses. These are amounts retained in years where experience is better than average to offset against the years where experience is worse than average.

Insurers must set aside money to pay for losses that already occurred, but also for losses not yet reported. This money is called a loss reserve.

The unearned premium reserves (UPR) are premiums that have already been paid but which relate to the next period. (See the example 2 on the next page)

Illustration 16: Technical reserves of a non-life insurance company

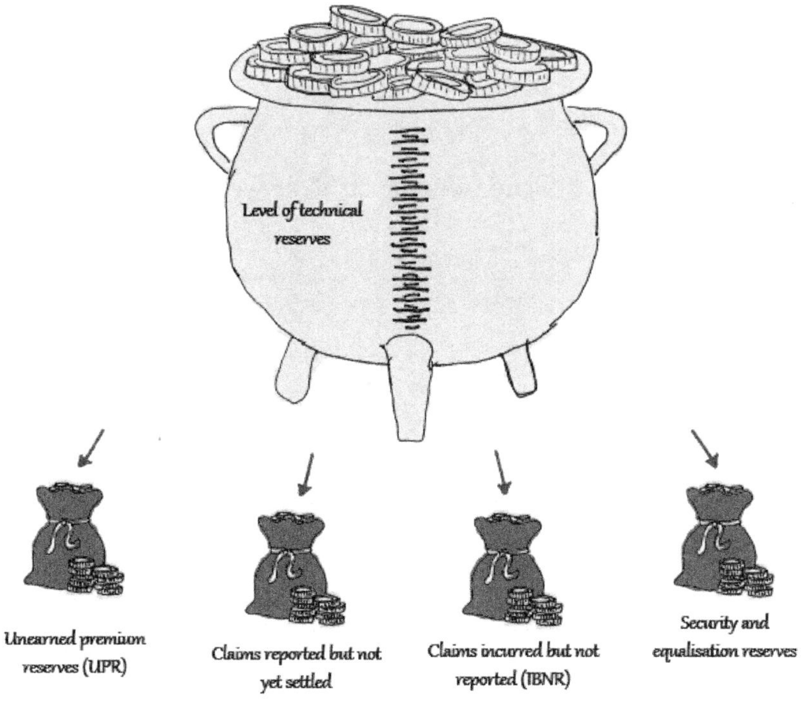

****

Example 2: Amy and InsuR - UPR

In our example, let's assume that Amy paid a premium of $1,200 on the 15th of April to InsuR to cover her property from the 1st of May until the 30th of April of the following year. She paid her premium in advance for a service to be provided by the insurer. InsuR is earning Amy's premium at a rate of $100 per month ($1,200/12). If Amy did cancel her policy after two months, then InsuR would have had to refund the premium relating for the ten months of insurance coverage minus a cancellation fee. So, within two months of the policy, the unearned premium is $1,000 ($1,200-$200).

****

Illustration 17: Unearned Premium Reserve

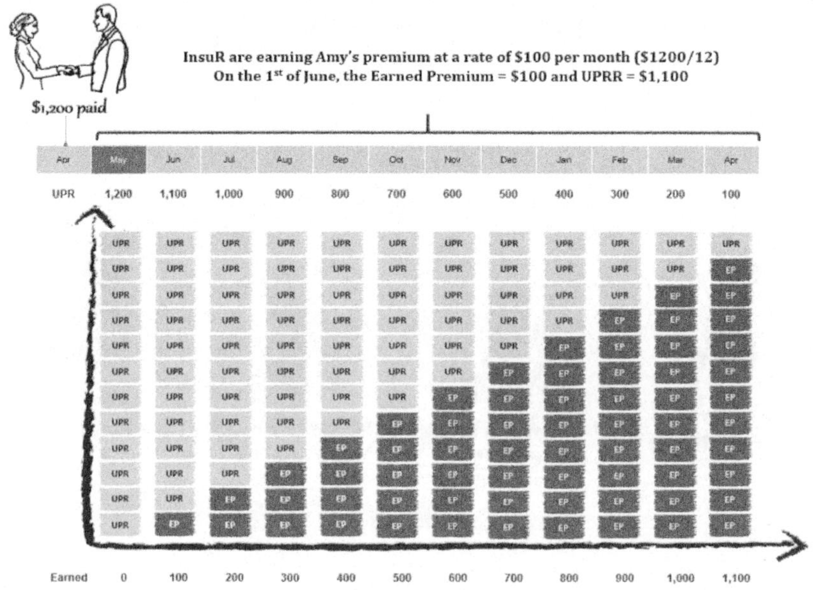

The unearned premium reserve is the insurer's liability for the in-force policies. Over time these unearned premiums are becoming "earned premium" which could be used to pay the claims under the policies and cover the insurer's costs (including the acquisition costs).

Insurers cannot use the money they collect in premiums immediately; they must wait until those premiums are earned. Unearned premiums must be held in an unearned premium reserve. Premium are earned on a pro rata basis throughout the term of a policy and cannot be fully earned until the policy expires.

In example 2, the $1,200 will not be earned on the 1st of May. Insur will report the $1,200 in its Cash account and should report $1,200 as a current liability in the account: Unearned Premium Reserve. As the premium is earned, the insurance company will move the amount earned from the liability account to a revenue account on its income statement.

An insurer that collects more money in premiums than it pays out in claims and expenses will run an underwriting profit. If an insurer pays more in claims and expenses that it collects in premiums, it will sustain an underwriting loss, but its overall results could still be positives.

Illustration 18: Underwriting profit and loss

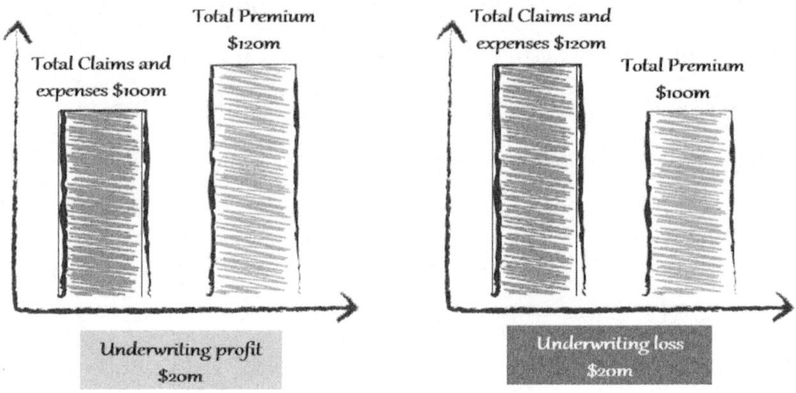

How could an insurer post a profit when its underwriting operations are running a loss?

The insurers are running two different activities: (i) the insurance underwriting activities described earlier (Premium pooling and claims payment) and (ii) the investment activities which generate an additional income when the collected premiums and claims reserves are invested.

Insurers invest in "safe" assets that can be converted to cash quickly to protect the policyholders (the insurers' clients) and meet all their obligations (mainly the payments of claims). The safe-haven assets such as bank deposits and fixed-income securities (debt instrument issued by a government, corporation or other entity) are the biggest asset class in the insurers' portfolios.

The proceeds of these investments enable the insurance companies to continue their insurance operations when underwriting losses exceed the amount collected from premiums (see the example 3 below)

****

Example 3: InsuR – Investment Income

Let's consider the following results of InsuR for the FY2016.

On the revenues side:

Premium Income	*$500m*
Investment Income	*$200m*
Total Revenues	*$700m*

On the expenses side:

Policyholder benefits and claims incurred	*$400m*
Policy acquisition and other expenses	*$200m*
Other expenses	*$40m*
Total benefits, claims and expenses	*$640m*

In 2016, InsuR earned $200 million in investment income and sustained a $140 million underwriting loss (Premium Income-total benefits, claims and expenses). With the help of a $200m investment income, InsuR still earned a profit of $60 million.

****

Insurers have two sources of income, underwriting (premiums less claims and expenses) and investment income. The investment income usually helps insurers to offset their underwriting losses.

Investment regulations are preventing insurers from making unsound investments that could threaten the company's solvency and harm the policyholders.

What are the insurers using to generate their investment income?

They are investing the money that they must keep on hand to pay the future claims/losses (and some expenses). It includes the unearned premiums (introduced earlier in this chapter), but the most significant portion of that money represents the reserves for future losses (e.g. the loss reserves including the IBNR).

This is what we called the "insurance float" or also insurance leverage.

Gollum

The beauty of the insurance float

What insurers are doing with the float is the equivalent of what banks are doing when they collect deposits. The banks are investing the deposits (through loans to other people or companies), and then repay the money when their client make a withdrawal or buy something. It is worth noticing that over the past ten years, the US Property and Casualty industry has been running a combined ratio close to 100% (only three years below 100%) (See the illustration 19 below).

Illustration 19: The combined ratio of the US property and casualty insurance industry over the past ten years

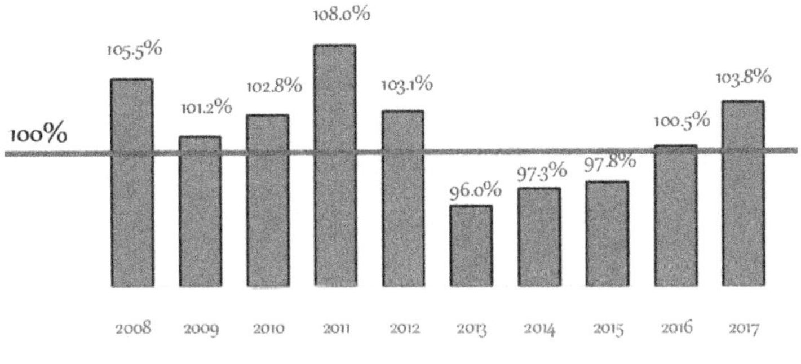

The float has been at the core of Berkshire's success (See chapter 10), and there is a lot to learn from Warren Buffett's annual letters.

In his 2002 Berkshire Hathaway Shareholder Letter, Warren Buffett explains:
"To begin with, the float is money we hold but don't own. In an insurance operation, float arises because premiums are received before losses are paid, an interval that sometimes extends over many years. During that time, the insurer invests the money. This pleasant activity typically carries with it a downside: The premiums that an insurer takes in usually do not cover the losses and expenses it eventually must pay. That leaves it running an "underwriting loss," which is the cost of float.

An insurance business has value if its cost of float over time is less than the expense the company would otherwise incur to obtain funds. But the business is a lemon if its cost of float is higher than market rates for money."

In his 2016 Berkshire Hathaway Shareholder Letter, we are getting even a much better view on how crucial is the float for insurers: "One reason we were attracted to the P/C business was its financial characteristics: P/C insurers receive premiums upfront and pay claims later. In extreme cases, such as claims arising from exposure to asbestos, payments can stretch over many decades. This collect-now, pay-later model leaves P/C companies holding large sums – money we call "float" – that will eventually go to others. Meanwhile, insurers get to invest this float for their own benefit. Though individual policies and claims come and go, the amount of float an insurer holds usually remains stable in relation to premium volume. Consequently, as our business grows, so does our float..."

Insurers which are operating with an underwriting profit, are effectively having a "cost-free" float.

With the example of InsuR, Quoting Warren Buffet, if InsuR were running an underwriting profit, then it would be as if someone deposited roughly $4bn with the insurer which managed to generate a $200m investment income without having to pay any interest to the depositor.

All the items covered in this chapter are interesting but how do we know if the size of the pot is accurate? This is what we will cover in the next chapter.

CHAPTER 3

THE DANGERS WITH THE INSURANCE RESERVES

What are the primary causes of failures for insurance companies?
What brought down a small liability insurer?
What lessons can we draw from it?

BY ERIC LEFEBVRE

Chapter Three

Reserving – a ticking time bomb challenge.

"Prediction is very difficult, especially if it's about the future."
— Niels Bohr

The one in 200 years: **Switzerland, August 2015**

As I am reading the Financial Times, I am learning about a massive explosion that took place in Tianjin, China. As the news kept coming, like others, I felt sorry for the people who perished.

After few days, we could see in the medias numerous illustrations of the destruction and I noticed the remarkable number of vehicles that were destroyed in the accident (not to mention the buildings and other facilities) and started wondering which insurers were the most exposed to this event.

Illustration 20: The aftermath of explosions in Tianjin, China, in 2015

Approximately 8,000 just-assembled cars awaiting shipment were destroyed in the explosion, as the photos show row after row of new Hyundais, Kias, Volkswagens, Renaults, Toyotas, and others scorched by the flames. Most likely the costs for these vehicles were only the tip of the iceberg.

It did not take long to discover the most hit insurers. In September 2015, Zurich Insurance warned that it faced significant losses after the Tianjin explosions. Because of this, it left out in the cold the British insurer RSA when it pulled out of a £5.6bn bid.

When they later announced their quarterly results, we learned that the industrial disaster costed the insurance provider, $275 million (€254 million).

Trouble comes in threes and in that quarter, Zurich confirmed this. Including the costs for Tianjin, the insurer posted after-tax profits of $207 million down from $966 million over the same period a year early, a decrease also linked to poor performance in its general insurance unit. In other words, the Tianjin explosion created a significant loss for Zurich, but other events hit them badly in 2016. The Swiss insurer also announced that they had to increase their reserves for their U.S. auto liabilities.

How could an insurer lose $750 million in a quarter?

In the case of Zurich, they were unfortunate to have a concentration of their risks in the same place in Tianjin thus a rather impressive hit as the result of the explosion. They also had to increase their reserves in the US for a part of their long tail businesses and this means that they experienced most likely a higher level of claims than anticipated when the policies were put in place.

The financial strength of Zurich and their skilled management team helped them to go through the storm and to even maintain their dividends for the Financial Year 2016.

A very different business model from those of other firms

As described earlier, the insurers are collecting from their customers the premium upfront and fulfil their payment obligations (deliver the product) only when a covered claim occurs. The other industries must market and sell a finished product before getting money from their customers. The insurers have an inverted production cycle. This inverted production cycle creates the float, thus the ability for insurers to earn an investment income on collected premium until having to pay a claim.

Etymology tells us that “premium” comes from Latin praemium with (i) prae meaning "before" (see pre-) and (ii) emere meaning "to buy”. “Premium” could mean “buy before” which is what customers do when they buy an insurance cover.

Getting paid before delivering a service brings opportunities (previous discussion on the float) but also challenges. The insurers should not recognise the total premium paid upfront as a full revenue, and they need to recognise it as the services are provided, thus the unearned premium concept which was described earlier. The earned premium is proportional to the coverage supplied over time.

Illustration 21: Payment before the delivery of a service

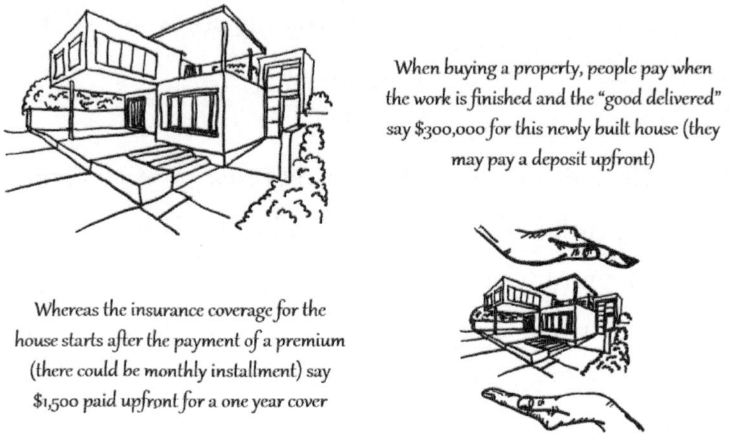

There are numerous counts of insurers that went insolvent by incorrectly accounting their earned premium. These insurers earned their premium "too early" in a manner that did not match the timing of claims under their policies. Their business appears to be very profitable during the early part of the coverage. When the claims were reported, the remaining assets were too low to cover the rapidly raising liabilities thus having these insurers becoming insolvent or announcing a loss.

The reserving challenges are especially real for multi-year general insurance policies where a single premium covers several years of risk. Some relevant examples of multi-year policies include builders warranty, consumer credit, mortgage insurance and tail cover for professional indemnity or medical malpractice (a tail cover is a provision that allows an insured to make claims after a policy has expired for acts that occurred while the policy was still valid).

Illustration 22: How works a tail coverage

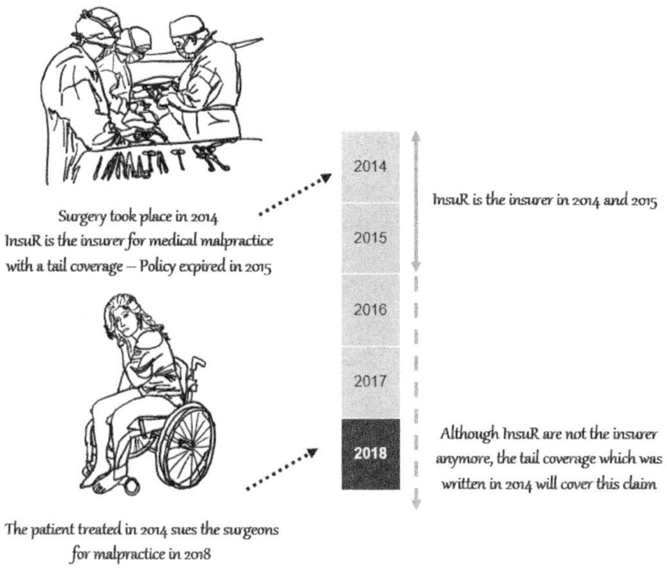

With tail covers, how should the insurer account the earned premium?

Let's assume that the insurance firm InsuR receives a $14,000 premium to cover the years 2014, 2015 plus a five years tail cover. The questions are: (i) how to split the $14,000? (ii) How much should be earned the first year and the following years? Should it be divided equally over seven years? (See the illustration 23 on the next page)

Illustration 23: Possible scenarios to earn the $14,000 premiums over seven years

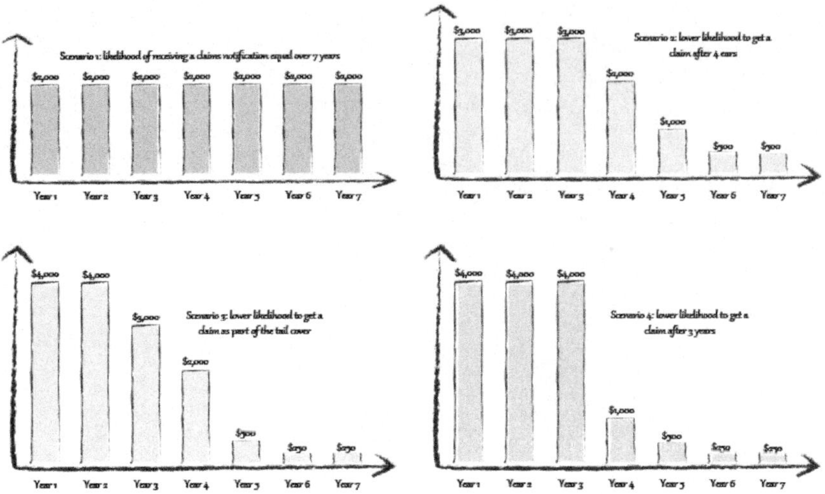

The insurers must come up with the right assumptions to earn the premiums adequately for their long tail businesses. Pursuing the wrong models could have dramatic consequences for the insurers.

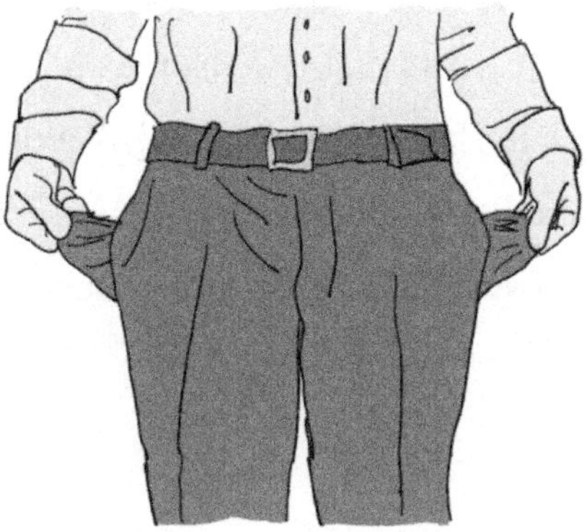

How would the insurer be able to pay the claims for insured events which have not yet occurred, if their "Unearned Premium Reserve" is too low?

When coming up with the Unearned Premium Reserve (UPR), the insurers are trying to estimate the outstanding liabilities (Claims and associated expenses) in the unexpired period of cover, e.g. the 2 + 5 years of coverage in our previous example.

The issue with the UPR is that it is calculated by taking a proportion of the collection premium (See illustration 23 on the previous page). If the collected premium is too low, a portion of it, won't be sufficient to cover the future claims.

To come up with their UPR, the insurers need to calculate the amount which needs to be set aside to cover the future claims and expenses, this is called the Unexpired Risk Reserve (URR). If the URR is higher than the UPR, the insurer needs to maintain an extra level of reserve, in the form of provision for premium deficiency. This extra level of reserve is often called the Additional Unexpired Risk Reserve (AURR)

To calculate the URR, the actuaries need to forecast the claims that are expected to occur in the future in relation to the unexpired exposure of a line of business (e.g. Medical malpractice), including the expected claims management expenses for that portfolio.

Therefore, the Insurer's Total Liabilities at any point in time are: (i) the outstanding claims reserves which include the "claims reported but not yet settled" and the "claims incurred but not yet reported" (IBNR) and (ii) the Unexpired Risk Reserve which contain the Claims not yet incurred but covered by the existing policies.

One could easily understand that it is tough to estimate future losses in long-tail lines (even if the insurers have lots of claims data at hand). The liability claims are less predictable than for example physical damage from car accidents.

Quoting "Warren Buffet", following the purchase of "Medical Protective Company (MedPro)" in 2006 by Berkshire Hathaway, "Malpractice insurance is tough to underwrite and has proved to be a graveyard for many insurers". Immediately after the purchase of MedPro, Berkshire increased its loss reserves by about $125 million. Excluding the added reserves for prior periods, MedPro wrote at an underwriting profit.

A long tail book of business which is "under reserved" could be a hidden ticking bomb in an insurer's portfolio. For years, the insurer could be posting underwriting profits and being optimistic about its future while troubles are brewing.

We can wonder how Dr Strangelove would describe this situation!

Why do insurers want to write long-tail lines?

As described in the previous chapter, an insurance company takes in premiums upfront and pays out claims later; it is, in effect, borrowing from its policyholders. Therefore, by nature, the long-tail lines create cheap long-term borrowing opportunities for insurance companies. This explains the success of Berkshire Hathaway which over time became the reinsurer of last resort, which reinsures businesses that other reinsurers would not touch, especially the long-tail business lines.

Lots of insurers have tried to repeat the success of Berkshire Hathaway by pursuing opportunities in long-tail lines. Some of them have unfortunately discovered that there is very little "Berkshire-quality" float existing in the insurance world.

For instance, in 2012, an international insurer reported that it added a $550 million pre-tax financial adjustment to its German general insurance business' long-tail liability reserves and deferred acquisition costs. This half a billion adjustment was related to medical malpractice and architects' and engineers' professional liabilities.

Because loss costs must be estimated, insurers have enormous latitude in figuring their underwriting results. Errors of estimation can be huge. The consequences of these miscalculations flow directly into the insurers' earnings.

With its big balance sheet and good portfolio diversification, Zurich insurance could weather the half a billion adjustment to its reserve in Germany, but the same could not be said for smaller insurers. It is worth reviewing the case of CBL insurance, a small insurer incorporated in New Zealand, which went into liquidation in 2018.

What happened with CBL insurance which was a promising "gazelle" in New Zealand?

At the beginning of 2018, CBL Corporation (the parent company) was a roaring New Zealand success story. It debuted on the New Zealand stock exchange in October 2015 at NZD1.73, and its share price rose to more than NZD3 in a couple of years. This was sustained by strong growth of its collected premium and their underlying earnings. Its managing director Peter Harris was also named EY Entrepreneur of the Year in 2017.

From 2009 until 2016, CBL insurance has been running a CAGR of 52% for its operating profit moreover, a CAGR of 40% for its net premium, clearly a rocket-fuelled growth (see the illustration 24 below).

Illustration 24: CBL Insurance – Financial Results from 2009 to 2016

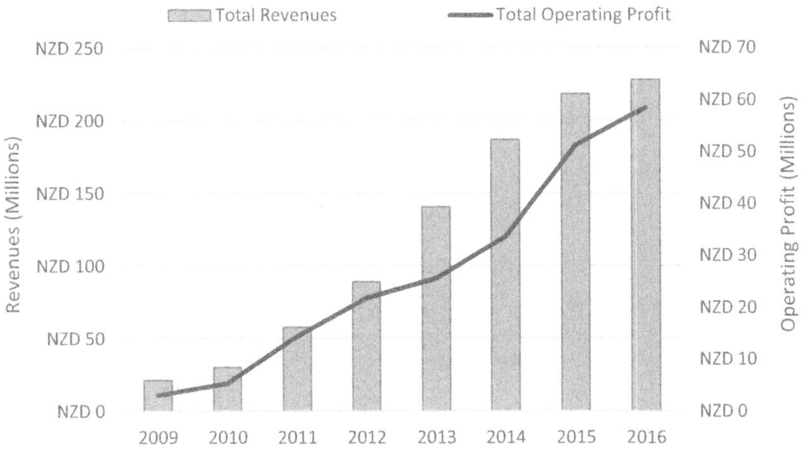

But at the beginning of 2018, CBL insurance announced that it had to strengthen the reserves for its long-tail French construction insurance business by NZD 100 million, and had made an NZD 44m write-off, resulting in a likely after-tax loss of between NZD 75m to NZD 85m for the FY2017, down from an operating profit of roughly NZD 60m a year earlier. It is interesting to notice that for many years their operating profit were approximately 25% of their total revenues which was an extraordinary performance when compared to other "more traditional insurers" (see the illustration 25 on the next page).

Illustration 25: Operating Margin % for a selection of insurers in 2016

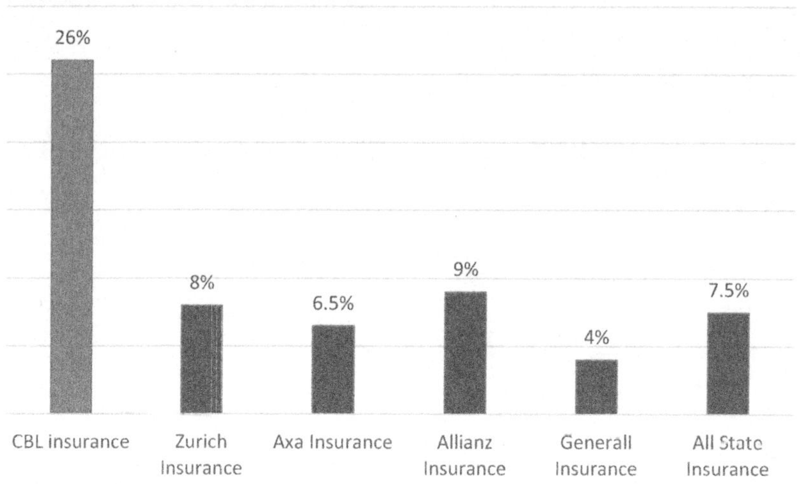

When the reported operating margin of an insurer far exceeds its peers while its operating expense and acquisition costs are within the norm, one should check this insurer's outstanding liabilities.

Back in the 1990s, A.M. Best carried out insightful research into why insurance companies fail. In 1999, they published the findings of their investigation into the failure of 640 US companies (from 1969 to 1998). Roughly two-thirds of the failures are the results of poor reserving policies or a low level of collected premiums (see table 5 below). These failures are often the results of poor management practices.

Table 5: Primary causes of failures for insurance companies in the US from 1969 to 1998

Primary reasons of failure	# of Companies	% of Total Identified
Insufficient Reserves	145	34%
Rapid Growth (Under Pricing)	86	20%
Alleged Fraud	44	10%
Overstated Assets	39	9%
Catastrophe Losses	36	8%
Significant Change in Business	28	7%
Impaired Affiliate	26	6%
Reinsurance Failure	22	5%
Total Identified	**426**	**100%**

Would some of these primary causes of failure explain what happened with CBL insurance?

At the time of writing this book, it seems that CBL insurance had under-reserving issues with some of its insurance businesses, especially its French operations which were conducting mainly construction insurance.

So, what went wrong with CBL insurance?

Just over 1% of CBL insurance business premium was in New Zealand, and its foreign business had been growing much faster than the NZ Business. A considerable share of their business related to builders' warranty and similar products (long-tail liabilities).

Its "French construction business" referred to builder's insurances in France which are mainly compulsory covers and provide protection for households or property owners, as well as for builders' liabilities for construction defects.

This cover is rather simple but the statutory claim notification period brings some complexity from an actuarial perspective. The period of cover is short, generally one year or the duration of the construction, but the claim notification period is extending for ten years. When adding the time to settle the claims and recover part of the losses (three years), the liabilities could last for more than 13 years after the issuance of a policy (see the illustration 26 on the following page).

Illustration 26: Builders' insurance system in France

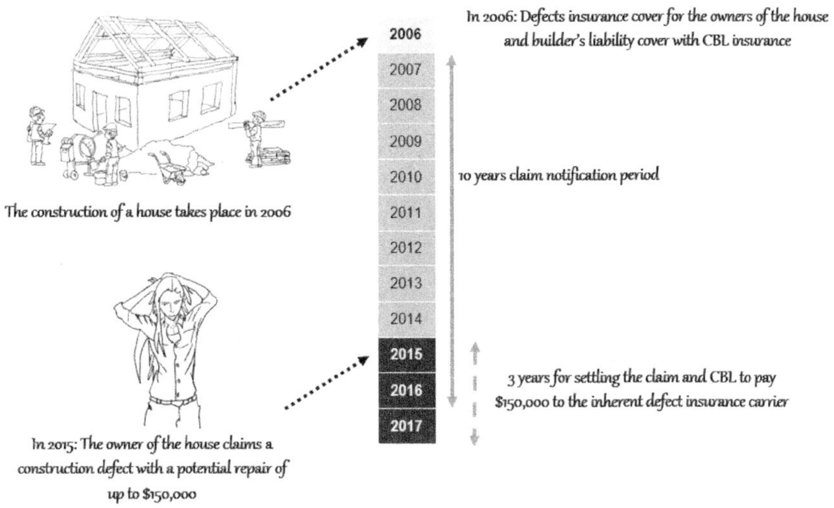

The French construction insurance system is a "double-barrelled" system: (i) the inherent defect insurance carrier compensates the property owner according to standard clauses and (ii) the intrinsic defect insurance carrier pursues damages against the builder and his liability insurers under decennial liability. This system allows the client to be compensated rapidly, and guarantees that the consumer will be protected.

CBL Insurance was offering three types of insurance in France:

1) The "dommages ouvrage" (Structural damage insurance) which refinances the cost of repairing defects which would appear after acceptance of the building and are covered by a ten-year warranty. These products cover the builders' clients, e.g. by law, a householder who wants to build a new house must buy such cover before having the builder to start the work. The insurer must indemnify the customer within three months and could recover from the builders' insurance cover called the "assurance decennale" (decennial liability insurance)
2) The "decennial liability insurance" covers the builders' risks (also called builders' warranty products). The "builders" are responsible to the client and successive buyers for the work they perform for ten full years. The date of Acceptance of Works marks the beginning of the period of responsibility. Construction costs can be significantly increased by the cost of insurance, which could be up to 1.5% of the basic value.

There are two subsets for the decennial liability insurance:

- the professional liability (Responsabilite civile professionelle) which covers the "builders" during the construction phase of the building or property,
- the decennial liability insurance covers the costs in the event of a total or partial collapse of the building, or some latent structural defects that compromise the building's safety and/or stability

Decennial liability insurance portfolios can have a pervasive impact on the balance sheet of an insurer. The consequences of wrong assumptions when setting the price for the products or putting aside assets could be felt long after the inception of the policies.

CBL Insurance's French business had grown significantly over the years with a compound annual growth rate (CAGR) in GWP of 46% from 2007 to 2016. The GWP was $1m in 2006, $38m in 2011 and $130m in 2016. The proportion of Decennial Liability insurance grew from 16% in 2007 to 33% in 2010 and finally 80% from 2014 onwards. The French Business GWP represented roughly 50% of the overall GWP for CBL Insurance.

Overtime CBL insurance got very exposed to Decennial liability insurance which are the riskiest products – roughly 40% of its global portfolio.

The percentage of total gross outstanding claims reserves that related to French business had grown from 0% when CBLI started the business in 2006 to 64% by the end of 2016. Over five years, total gross outstanding claims reserves had increased from $10m at the end of 2011 to $223m at the end of 2016. The net outstanding claims reserves had risen from $8m at the end of 2011 to $151m at the end of 2016.

The announcement in 2018 of the need to further strengthen the reserve by $100m means that the net outstanding claims reserves were most likely well above $300m for the French Business. It seems that CBLI's financials were deteriorating very fast whereas the French business had not yet reached the end of the claiming period for even their oldest underwriting year.

The outstanding claims reserve represents the loss liabilities for insurance claims which have been reported and not yet settled (RBNS) or which have been incurred but not yet reported (IBNR) reserves. This is a technical reserve of an insurance company and is established to provide for the future liability for claims which have occurred but not been settled.

An increase of $100m to the outstanding loss reserve in France means that for years, CBL underestimated their potential exposures to their builders' warranty insurance portfolio. Most likely, the collected premiums were earned too quickly, and the loss ratios were underestimated for a growing portfolio.

In February 2018, the CEO of CBL Insurance declared to its New Zealand regulator that the company's solvency margin was below 100%, it was still at 150% back in July 2017 (See table 6 on the following page).

The solvency margin is a minimum excess on an insurer's assets over its liabilities set by regulators. It can be regarded like the capital adequacy requirements for banks and act as a buffer. Its purpose is to ensure that an insurance company has additional funds above its reserves to cover fluctuations in its claims experience. These funds (called required capital) consist of shareholder capital plus free reserves, which are the results of retained profits from the past.

Table 6: Solvency capital CBL insurance from 06/2016 until 06/2017

In $'000	30/06/2017 Readjusted in Oct 2017	30/06/2017	31/12/2016	30/06/2016
Actual Solvency Capital	160,440	160,440	153,086	133,314
Minimum Solvency Capital	121,174	106,800	81,173	79,309
Solvency Margin	39,266	53,640	71,913	54,005
Solvency Ratio	**132%**	**150%**	**189%**	**168%**

Illustration 27: Typical Solvency II Balance Sheet

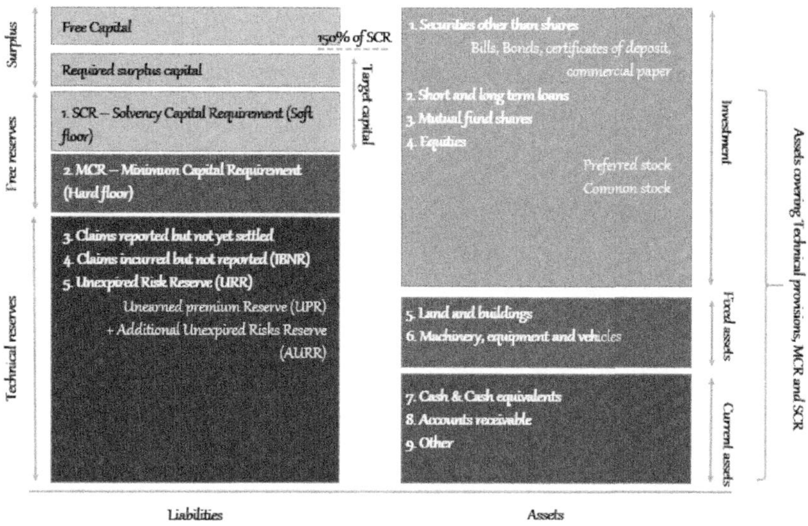

What does it mean when the solvency margin is below 100%?

If the capital adequacy ratio is lower than 100%, the insurer can still in principle fulfil its current and future payment guarantees. The company must then take steps to achieve a capital adequacy ratio of more than 100%. A solvency ratio below 100% is not an indication of bankruptcy, it means that the safety buffer for extreme crisis scenarios is no longer met in full.

Depending on the countries, the regulators may react differently when the solvency margin of an insurer falls below 100%.

For instance, with regards to the solvency margin, the China Insurance Regulatory Commission (the "CIRC") follows a three-tier structure:

1) A solvency level above 150% is considered "met" and the insurers are "Adequate II"
2) The insurers with a solvency ratio between 100% to 150% are "Adequate I", and the CIRC can request them to come up with an insolvent prevention plan
3) delinquent insurers with a solvency ratio below 100% would result in the harshest sanction as they are deemed to be "Inadequate".

For instance, in 2018, Anbang Insurance Group was taken over by its insurance regulator and the Chinese government had to inject roughly 10 $billion. Its chairman was put on trial on fraud charges in the aftermath of this rescue.

In the Netherlands, when an insurer does not meet the 100% threshold, the Nederlandsche Bank (DNB) has several options for intervention. One of them is requiring insurers to submit a recovery plan. Such recovery plans, subject to DNB's assessment and approval, should help the insurer to meet the requirement again within six months. The DNB may appoint a secret receiver, impose a production stop or revoke the insurer's authorisation. DNB may also transfer insurance portfolios and adjust the policy conditions.

This is what happened for CBLI in New Zealand, where the high court ordered in late February 2018, the insurer to be placed into interim liquidation.

CBL is a double whammy story

The deterioration in the solvency ratio of CBL (as per table 6) was linked to a significant increase of its "Minimum Solvency Capital" showing that the buffer was slimmer than thought with rapid deterioration.

Why the MSC increased or had to be revised upwards?

Like for most insurance solvency models, (the one from the Reserve Bank of New Zealand is no exception), the underwriting risk, which represents loss reserves and premiums written, is the primary driver of required capital (roughly 50% of total capital requirements).

In France, the significant increase in the loss reserve of CBL meant a massive expansion to the MSC.

When an insurer gets its technical provision wrong, there is a "double whammy" which can take place as the capital will equally be wrong. An impact to the loss reserve (high increase) would amplify the effect to the excess of own funds.

What happened to the customers of CBL insurance?

In March 2018, Independent building warranty provider Stamford Insurance said, it has stepped in with a new scheme to protect the NZ clients of CBL Insurance. With the help of Lloyd's of London, Stamford put in place an insurance scheme to protect both buyers and homeowners who were clients of CBL Insurance:

- For buyers who have signed a contract and paid a deposit where work has yet to start, Stamford would cover the risk that they may lose their deposit if their builder becomes insolvent.
- If construction has already begun, Stamford will guard against builder insolvency and provide ten years' defects cover on completion.
- For homeowners who have taken possession of their homes within the past twelve months and who may have lost their protection against significant defects arising with their home, Stamford will offer them a new ten-year policy.

Could the management have avoided such debacle earlier?

At the beginning of 2018, for their French business, CBL Insurance had to significantly increase their claims reserve which means that most likely for many years their actuarial models underestimated their claims outstanding liabilities (e.g. its provisions for claims incurred but not reported - IBNR) and we could also wonder if CBL Insurance were earning their premiums too quickly.

With long tail liability insurance, the main challenge for insurers is to decide the period of risk over which to calculate the amount unexpired is not always easy.

For instance, the earning period for CBLI's builders' warranty insurance can be (i) over the course of construction but also (ii) over the construction period plus ten years.

In the case (i), any claims arising over the next ten years are linked to work carried out during the construction and are captured in the outstanding claims liability.
Whereas in the case (ii) a portion of the premium is earned during the period of construction and a portion of the premium is also earned over the following 10-year period.

The main question that insurers are facing is whether to allocate the collected cash to (i) an outstanding claims liability (based on historical data) or (ii) an unearned premium liability.

The risk margins for premium liabilities (roughly 27% on average) are much higher than those for the outstanding claims (12% on average). As a result, when following the first approach, an insurance company would have higher total insurance liabilities.

When an insurance company earn premiums too quickly, the loss ratios will appear as being lower than what it should be. And the assumptions for the outstanding claims liabilities will be misleading, the insurer would end up underestimating its claims liabilities.

CBL Insurance followed the 1st approach (Allocation of cash to an outstanding claim liability) and was earning its premium as follow: 4.2% in the first month then 8.3% in each of the following months (two to twelve) and then 4.2% in the thirteenth month. This could potentially explain why the operating margin was so high.

When looking back at the financial results, the missing $100m could have easily been put aside over ten years, but CBL insurance would have had to pay a lower dividend.

What have we learned so far?

The financial operations of an insurer are to be viewed in terms of a series of cash inflows (income) and outflows (payments).

The inflow components are added to the pot of assets, while the reserve is depleted by the outflow components.

The Insurers must ensure that at anytime their pot never get empty (dry), in order words, they must remain solvent (see the illustration 28 on the following page)

The main inflow components for an insurer are:

- The premiums which are the primary incomes
- The income from investments (e.g. interest payments, dividends, rents from own properties, gains from assets such as shares, etc)
- The recoveries of claims from reinsurers (when an insurer transfer some its risks or parts of risk to a reinsurer
- The issuance of new capital to shareholders

The main outflow components for an insurer are:

- The payments for claims
- The reinsurance premiums (Thus the recoveries of claims described earlier)
- The expenses which cover the commissions paid to the distributors, the administration and operating costs
- The taxes paid when realising a profit
- The dividends paid to shareholders (or surplus for a mutual insurance company) and the bonuses paid to policyholders (when profit-sharing schemes are in place)

Illustration 28: The insurance cauldron

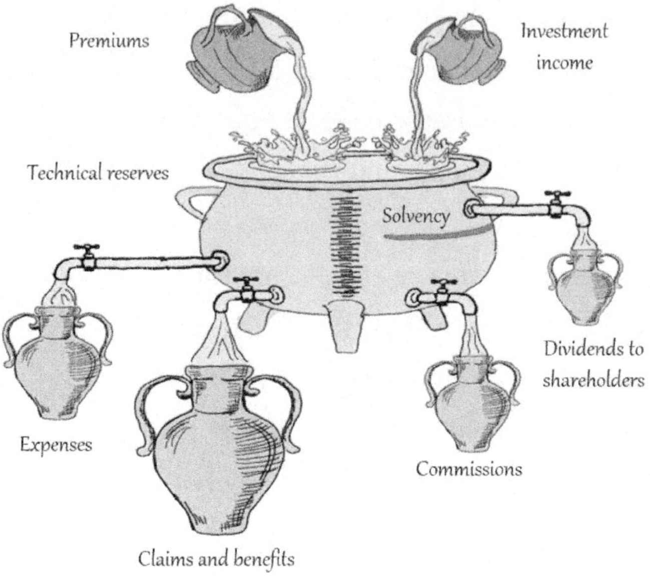

As seen with the example of CBL Insurance, the consequences of under-reserving could be dramatic for an insurer, especially for the monoline insurers. Strengthening of reserves for prior accident years or lack of premium reserves can significantly reduce the companies' earnings, pretty much what happened to Zurich insurance in 2016. The difference between Zurich insurance and CBL insurance is that Zurich enjoys significant diversification advantages with business in several product lines and geographies.

Regulators have imposed the solvency risk model to ensure that Insurers have the necessary "buffers" to be better able to withstand significant losses and unknowns. However, the insurers need to come up with the right premiums to cover the risks of their clients. This is what we will cover in the next chapter.

CHAPTER 4

THE INSURANCE PRICING AND ITS CHALLENGES

How do insurers calculate a rate?
What are the challenges when pricing new risks such as cyber?
Do insurers have a good memory?

BY ERIC LEFEBVRE

Chapter Four

Pricing - The enigma of insurance

"If everyone is thinking alike, then somebody isn't thinking."
— George S. Patton Jr.

My introduction to the "proper rate": Europe, early 2006

Following the success of packaged General Insurance Products (Property & Casualty, Business Interruption, Liability, D&O, Identity theft) sold to SMEs (Small & Medium sized entities) in the UK, we decided to launch similar products across several European countries. The vision was to have a simplified onboarding process (with a maximum of five questions asked to clients) and use a web-based platform opened to distributors (brokers) for quoting and issuing the policies (binding the policies).

The same platform was to be used for opening and settling claims. Adding to the complexity of building such products and the platform, we also needed to come up with a new organisation to manage the end to end process.

This was a significant undertaking for an Insurer which "core business" was to cover and serve very large corporation and did not have the capacity nor the "know-how" to enter what we would call the "small and middle market".

Effectively the ambition was to move from an organisation running processes to sell and manage "tailor-made products" to an organisation with industrialised processes to serve a "mass market".

With some hurdles, we managed to resolve the technical challenges and set-up the "factory" not to mention the possibility to issue a full quote and bind a policy based on five questions. However, the biggest challenge was to come up with the right pricing!

The rates which were used in Europe by this insurer were for significant risks thus being inadequate for our target market. We followed classic cost based actuarial techniques (premiums based on anticipated losses and expenses) but were still far from the market practices.

This was when I learned that prices are not solely based on actuarial calculation. To be competitive and furthermore enter the market, we had to deviate a lot from our theoretical rates and follow the Marketplace pricing (supply & demand forces). To come up with the "proper rate", we hired some underwriters from the competition with the necessary market knowledge. We finally tested our pricing with "friendly" brokers to further calibrate our packages.

When trying to understand why the market was so far than the "theoretical rates", I realised that we were in the middle of a very soft market and decided to understand the "underwriting cycle" better.

Today you can find an enormous number of articles trying to explain the underwriting cycle. Most of these articles attribute the cycles to economic factors, more specifically the availability of capital but is it all about this?

Before covering the market forces, let's first define what is the purpose of an insurance premium or rate?

Back in 1950, C. A. Kulp already defined the insurance premium or rate as being the price charged for an insurance cover. This price should allow an insurer to collect enough funds to cover its obligation under the contract (future liabilities) and should also distribute the cost of insurance equitably among insured persons (pretty much the principle of mutualisation described in our first chapter). This definition is still relevant today with the first criteria being nowadays the "primary" objective of a premium.

Insurers are not different than any other business as the price charged to a customer should reflect the costs associated with the product as well as cover an acceptable profit margin.

The price or rate is equal to Cost plus Profits

Price = Costs + Profits

To summarise, a premium (price charged to a customer) should be sufficient to meet the future losses and cover the insurer expenses: its administration and acquisition costs (e.g. the commission paid to a broker), the principal obligation of an insurer being to remain solvent.

An insurer running an "underfunded" scheme could almost be a Ponzi scheme, if they use the premium collected from the new customers to pay for the claims of previous customers. The customers are never considering that their insurer would default and not be able to pay for their future damages.

What are the mechanisms for setting up a proper rate?

As defined earlier, the insurance premiums are based on the anticipated losses (prediction gained on experience) and expenses. The actuaries who are setting up the prices for the insurance products are using cost-based approaches, and estimate the future costs of providing the insurance cover.

As we know it, the main difference between selling insurance and selling other goods is that the actual cost of providing the protection is unknown until the end of the policy thus the need for the actuaries to come up with accurate projections for the insurance companies to be able to fulfil their obligations while being profitable.

To achieve that, most rates are determined by statistical analysis of past losses but also by adjusting these rates regularly to reflect the loss experience.

How do you come up with a rate when there is a lack of historical data?

We will use Cyber Insurance as an example to illustrate this challenge and furthermore highlight the potential risks for an insurer (and its shareholders) but also the policyholders. We will introduce some key elements required to understand the basic actuarial concepts and techniques for setting up the insurance rates.

Although Cyber Insurance has been around for almost two decades, the market is still immature. Some of the insurance players are facing their own built “causality dilemma” (especially the European insurers). On the one hand, the insurers are finding it very difficult to measure and control the cyber risks, and on the other hand, the clients are finding the products being very expensive with limited covers.

The issue is that the European Insurers must gain a better understanding of loss potential and coverage – They have a lack of historical data, making it difficult to build reliable predictive models. We are in the middle of a chicken or the egg causality dilemma.

One possible solution to resolve this loop is to come back to one of the core insurance principle: the pooling of risks. Although some people in the insurance industry may believe that "pricing risk and providing a cover to a customer" is an art, the basis for much of today's insurance evolved from the law of large numbers. Statistically, whenever a potentially random event is predicted, the more events recorded or tested, the more likely the outcome will match the predictions. Therefore, insurers must build up a risk pool to ensure the frequency distribution of their actuarial prediction but also constantly adjust their rates based upon the occurrence of losses.

There are several approaches for estimating the rates: (i) the pure premium method, (ii) the loss ratio method, (iii) a combination of both approaches and finally (iv) the judgment making method where underwriters determine rates primarily based on their experience and judgment.

However, before detailing some of these approached, we need to introduce the concept of exposure.

What is exposure?

As we described in previous chapters, to justify the need for an insurance cover, there needs to be an exposure to a loss. If there is no likelihood of a loss, there is no need for insurance. An insurance cover is a risk transfer, therefore from a client's perspective, the price for transferring the loss to a third party must represent a proportion of the expected loss. In other words, we must identify an exposure base. The "exposure unit" needs to be "reasonable", easy to determine and have historical practice.

The basic rating unit for an insurance premium is called an exposure. The unit of exposure is based upon the characteristics of the insurance coverage involved. For insurance, for car insurance, a car year exposure is one automobile insured for twelve months.

For auto collision insurance, one unit might by $1,000 worth of the value of the vehicle; for auto liability, a unit might be 100 kilometres driven. For liability coverage for a shop, units could be the number of customers. The insurance premium is the result of the amount of exposure units time the rate per unit.

For the collision coverage, the rate per unit could be $15 per unit with an exposure unit of $1,000 of car value. So, for a car worth $35,000, the premium is $15 time 35, or $525. If the customer appears as having a higher risk than others (e.g. a loss which took place within the three previous years), the insurer raises the rate per unit and this leads to a higher premium to be paid, e.g. a new rate at \$20 per unit which means a new premium at \$20 time 35, or \$700.

For Cyber insurance, the most significant risk for the insured are the loss of their clients' data. We could consider the costs associated with these losses as the exposure (Costs to inform the clients, investigate and remediate the breach, costs to reissue new credit cards). For instance, we could have a \$1 premium for \$1,000 exposure (costs associated with losing several client's data) which would mean the probability of losing data set at 1%.

What is a pure premium?

The pure premium covers the portion of the premium that is allocated towards claims. The term "pure" refers to the expected value of the insurance policy, which represents the average loss per unit of exposure (excluding the profits and other loads).

In an overly simplified model, we could consider the number of insured and check the total costs for claims.

For instance, let's say that in 2017, for its Cyber insurance portfolio for German SMEs, InsuR paid out \$10,000,000 in claims (including expenses) for 5,000 SMEs, the pure premium would then be \$2,000.

We could also say that one SME holds data on average for 2,000 customers. Therefore, the whole insurance pool would cover the risks of data loss for 10,000,000 clients. If we consider the exposure as being the # of customers for the SMEs, then the pure premium would be the total claims paid out divided by the # of customers. $10,000,000 divided by 10,000,000 customers which gives a pure premium of $1 per end customer (see the illustration 29 below).

The pure premium is the average loss per unit of exposure. The formula for the pure premium is: P = L / E - Where: P = pure premium; L = losses; E = exposure units.

Illustration 29: Examples pure premium for cyber insurance

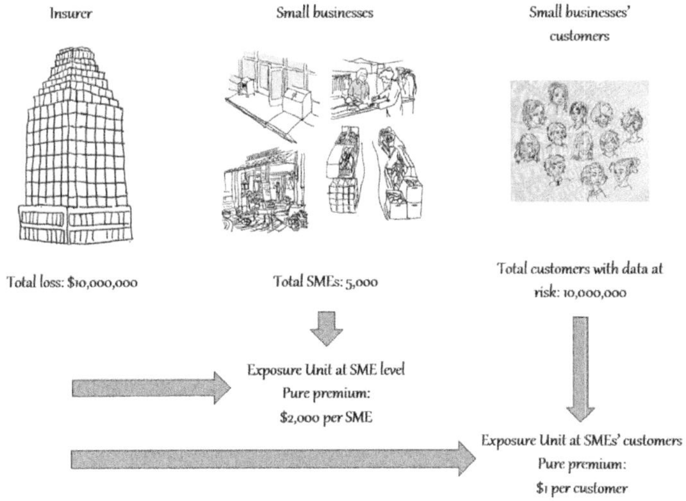

From pure premium to gross premium

To come up with the gross premium for cyber coverage (charged to the customer), there is a need to make the necessary provisions for the future expenses (other than the loss adjustment expenses already included in the pure premium) and profit. The required provisions could be a "loading ratio" and is added on top of the pure premium. It covers the administration and selling costs but also the desired profit for the insurer.

The Gross Premium Rate per unit of exposure is:

G = (P + F) / (1 – E – Q)

Where P is the pure premium, F the fixed expenses per exposure, E the variable expense load (sales + administration costs) and Q the profit factor.

For our previous example, we will assume a loading ratio of 30% (20% for expenses (E) + 10% for profit (Q)) and $0.15 for the other fixed costs (F).

Thc gross premium would then be calculated as follow:

G = ($1 + $0.15) / (1 - 0.3) = $1.64

What is the loss ratio method?

With this approach, the new rate for a class of business is determined by comparing the total actual loss costs with the expected costs.

The comparison is used to adjust the current insurance rate either upward or downward to reflect changing loss experience.

In our previous cyber example, the insurer Insur paid out in 2017, $10,000,000 in claims (including expenses) for 5,000 SMEs covered. If the SMEs paid on average a premium of $2,500, then the total collected premium would have been $12,500,000 thus a 2017 loss ratio of 80%.

Loss Ratio = Total Claims / Total Premium = 80%.

If InsuR determined to have a loss ratio of 75% in 2017, then they had a deficit and the insurance pricing for the year 2018 had to increase by 6.66%.
Premium increase or decrease = (Actual loss ratio – expected loss ratio) / Expected loss ratio = (80% - 75%) / 75%. = 6.66%

The loss ratio method seeks rate changes based on claims experience. The claims experience provides an adjustment factor which is used to update the premium rate.
Indicated Rate = Adjustment Factor x Current Rate
Adjustment factor = experience loss Ratio / expected loss Ratio

When applied to a standard set of information, we know that the pure premium method and the loss ratio method are producing the same results, but what would be the best approach for Cyber insurance?

The main difference between the two approaches is that the pure premium method indicates rates whereas the loss ratio method provides adjustments to the rates.

What are the constraints with these two approaches?
The pure premium method requires well-defined exposures as it is based on losses per unit exposure.
The loss ratio method cannot be used for a new line of business as it requires an established rate and premium history.

The theory is interesting but how are the insurers tackling the current cyber insurance challenges?

Initially, cyber insurance focused on the third-party liabilities connected with data and privacy breaches, including notification costs, pretty much what we described in our previous examples. This was linked to breach notification laws, enacted in most US states, which mandate firms subject to data breaches to notify their customers and other parties about the breach, and to take the necessary measures to limit the potential damage caused to their customers.

Whereas, in Europe, insurers focused on the direct costs of a cyber-attack to their client, also named first-party costs. The first-party claim scenarios could be the malicious destruction of data, the denial of service attack, virus, malware, and spyware but also the cyber extortion threats.

Today most of the cyber insurance products cover first-party costs and third-party liability.

The insurers are pricing their client's risks against the following criteria:

- Company size and Turnover
- Indemnity limits, deductibles,
- Industry, as a proxy for risk exposure (e.g. the healthcare industry is much more exposed to cybercriminals than other sectors)
- Market exposure to other jurisdictions (especially the US)
- Assessment of IT and data security based on filled forms, interviews, or independent IT audits (including penetration testing)

What are the cyber insurance costs for small businesses?

It the United States, the annual premium ranges from $1,000 for most small businesses, up to $7,500 or more for mid-sized firms with higher revenue and a more significant number of client records.

Table 7: Premium and coverage limit per type of small business in the US

Business Type	Annual Premium	Annual Revenue	Coverage Limit
IT Provider for healthcare	$1,000	$500,000	$1,000,000
Healthcare Clinic	$1,200	$400,000	$1,000,000
CPA/Tax Preparation	$1,200	$100,000	$1,000,000
Small Retail Store	$1,100	$250,000	$1,000,000

Small companies see their annual premiums average around $1,000 for $1 million coverage limit (0.1% of coverage limit). Small businesses with higher revenue and a higher number of personal records kept, could pay premiums closer to the US average of $7,500.

In Europe, the premium paid for small businesses could span from 0.2% to 1.5% of the indemnity limit (€2000 to 15,000€ for €1 million coverage limit). In 2017, the London based insurer Sciemus (Occam Underwriting) was charging around $100,000 for $10 million in data breach insurance and as much as seven times that to cover attacks causing physical damage.

It seems that the Insurers are basing their pricing on expert models rather than on historical data and we could guess that some insurers may base their rates on rules of thumb.

Currently, the insurers are enjoying high margins with cybersecurity policies. Globally, the market could surpass $25 billion by 2025.

The industry is currently growing by 35% every year. With such growth, companies like AIG, Travelers, Chubb, and XL have rushed in and premiums are competitive. These four insurers lead in market share, with around 45% of the cyber policy market, says Fitch Ratings.

However, the future might not be so rosy. As stated in our previous chapters, the main risks for insurers are that the price of future claims is unknown when a customer buys a cover. Pricing is determined and agreed to before costs are known. Actuarial models and analysis are used to estimate the expected frequency and severity of future claims, but the future costs are unknown at the issuance of the policy (this is the "inverted production cycle" described in our previous chapter).

Why does this matter for cyber insurance?

We can find lots of reports stating that the cyber insurance product lines are highly profitable for insurers, with a combined ratio as low as 80%.

With new entrants getting into these "profitable" lines of business, we can already assume that in most markets the current premiums are below the actuarially fair premium.

For insurance to be actuarially fair, the premium rate must equal the probability of an accident, as stated earlier, there is a lack of data and claims experience thus having insurers pricing cyber risks without knowing the likelihood of loss, which is an issue when you are in an inverted production cycle…

Like many of their clients, the insurers are having difficulties in understanding the causes and impacts of large-scale cyber-attacks but also to anticipate where the next one might come from or how big it will be. One could only expect a disaster to happen as no one in the industry knows the risk.

There are in this lots of similarities with natural catastrophes such as hurricanes. Some researchers warn catastrophic cyber event triggering thousands of policyholders to file claims simultaneously could lead to insurers going insolvent, like in 1992 after Hurricane Andrew. Back then, insurers earned lots of money for almost twenty years insuring against catastrophic storms, with full confidence in their risk models. Over that period storms took place but there were not catastrophic storms, the insurers were not smart, they had been lucky. With Andrew, eleven insurers in the US went insolvent.

Warren Buffet said that cyber risk is part of his estimate that every year carries about a 2% chance of a super catastrophe that would cause $400 billion or more of insured losses.

In an interview with the financial times, Stephen Hester, chief executive of UK based RSA, had similar views. “We have mixed feelings about cyber insurance”. “Our job is to protect clients from things they are worried about, but it is incredibly unpredictable.” In their article, they also mentioned the case of one executive who went further. He said the system of annual policies is ill-suited to a risk that changes so quickly. He predicted that cyber insurance is “a disaster waiting to happen” for those who do not fully understand what is at stake.

Actuaries indicate rates, but the market sets prices.

Having their pricing right is crucial for insurers at least from an actuarial perspective, we know by now that in a very soft market, some insurers tend to “under-price” the risks to remain competitive and defend their market position.

These insurers are moving away from the “underwriting discipline” and embrace, if possible, the “cash flow underwriting”.

As part of the "cash flow underwriting", the insurers write the policies at a loss to collect premiums for investment thus relying on the float to generate a "hopefully" generous investment income. This works if interest rates are high, as it was the case in the 1970s, 80s and to a certain extent 1990s (see illustration 28 below). However, in a post-2008 financial crisis, with meagre interest rates, we all know that investment incomes are not sufficient for compensating the underwriting losses, thus insurers having to go back to basics (underwriting and cost discipline).

Illustration 30: US FED Funds interest rate % from 1954 to 2018

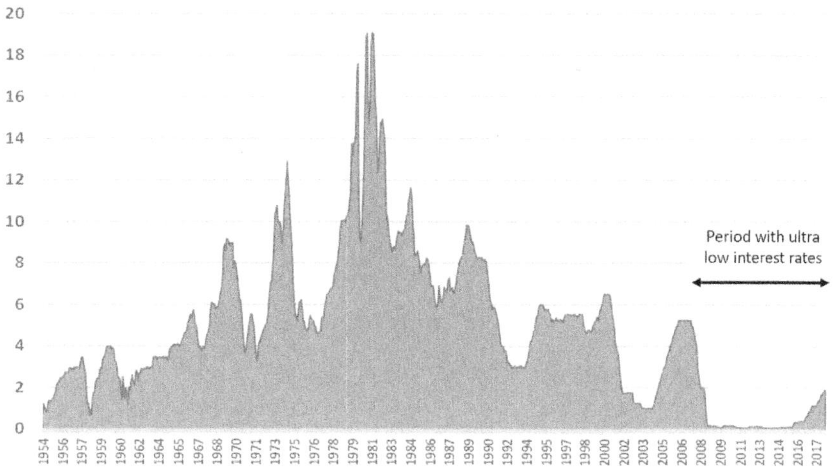

As described earlier in this book, insurers must maintain enough assets and capital to cover their liabilities. Like any balance sheet driven institutions such as banks or lenders, they are using the money which seats on their balance sheet as the raw material for their operations. Banks are using the capital made available to them (the deposits) and lend it to other firms or individuals whereas insurers are using the collected premiums for paying claims (which is the core of their business) and their operating expenses (which is the equivalent of a management fee applied to a pool of cash).

Insurers' insolvency arises when their assets and capital are insufficient to cover their claims liabilities (e.g. CBL insurance) or when a catastrophic event hit them (Hurricane Andrew in 1992). Most of the time when an Insurer goes insolvent, it is due to an inappropriate reserve, with the difficulties in risk pricing being often the cause.

Although this is at the core of Insurance, estimating the right prices is a very difficult and "dangerous activity". Entering new markets or lines of business (such as cyber insurance) heighten the risks even for experienced insurers.

In a recent report, Fitch Ratings urged insurers to take a cautious approach to underwrite cyber risk. "The evolving nature of events and uncertainty regarding the source and range of potential losses add further challenges,"

In our previous chapters, we described the needs for insurers to ensure that at anytime their "reservoir" or "cauldron" never get empty. To do so, they must maintain the right level of reserves (premium and claims) to weather future storms, but they also need to make sure that the collected premiums are accurately representing the written risks.

The hurricane Andrew in 1992 was a "wake-up" call for the industry with regards to "collecting the right premium" but also managing their risk exposure.

Insurers must diversify and spread their risk. For instance, in property insurance, they have learned to not concentrate too many policies within the same area (In 2015, Zurich insurance had a painful reminder of this basic in Tianjin, when a catastrophic explosion costed them $275m)
However, it seems that in a quest for growth and profits, with Cyber insurance, insurers may have forgotten some of the basics in terms of risk aggregation or the need to at least collect the actuarial premium.

With all the unknowns surrounding constantly evolving cyber risks, a meagre combined ratio should not be seen as an opportunity, it might be the calm before the storm or just pure luck.

Once, one analyst told me that he does not understand why some insurers are publishing heavy losses when a major event hits them. This should not be a surprise for them since "predicting" these events are at the core of their competencies, if they are not able to do so, people should not invest in them.

He was a bit extreme in his comments although I tend to agree with his overall views. I would add to this that we should not blindly rely on the solvency ratio and insurers' annual reports. As described in this chapter and earlier with the CBL, following wrong assumptions for pricing and reserving could have disastrous consequences regardless of having an excellent solvency ratio. One needs to carefully check an insurance company before investing in it or even work for it.

We have covered how non-life insurance firms work and what is at the core of their business model. It is time to review the other part of the insurance business: the business model of life insurance companies.

CHAPTER 5

THE CORE OF LIFE INSURANCE

What is the business model for life insurance?
How do life insurers win against the odds?
Are there any hidden secrets?

BY ERIC LEFEBVRE

Chapter Five

The numbers game

"When it is a question of money, everybody is of the same religion."
— Voltaire

Realising what life insurance is all about: France, fall 1998

Martine, my assistant, prepared the file for Mr Paul, our system gave us the 360-degree view of the customer, history, policies, claims and relatives. This was one of the last time I went to visit one client of our agency as I was getting ready to start my new job in Paris. Their house in the outskirts of Longwy looked small from outside and rather common, but I got surprised when inside. Everything was in the back and was invisible from thc street. The house was huge with big rooms and amazing Le Corbusier furniture and Ludwig Mies van der Rohe chairs. I met his wife who seemed younger than my client, and we went quickly to Mr Paul's office.

They offered me an excellent coffee and his wife left us to discuss all their insurance policies. Our client wanted to review his life insurance policies and was enquiring about transforming them in annuities for his wife in the case of his death. There were three life insurance policies, one term life with a sum insured of Fr1.5m and two unit-linked policies for a total of Fr2m. We reviewed the contracts and came up with options to convert the capital into annuities for his wife in the event of his death, which was rather easy to do, we agreed the next steps and engaged in a discussion about life in general.

Mr Paul was interested in my story and gave me some advice, as I left him, I had a strange feeling. Back in the office, Martine provided me additional information, our client married his secretary and did not have any kids, he was wealthy and a nice person, but he was in the final stage of cancer thus his enquiries. We did what he asked us to do for the annuities although I did not agree that it was in the best interest of his wife. A few months later while working in Paris, I received a call from Martine who informed me that our client passed away.

This is when I decided to check further how Life Insurance Company earn money knowing that their insured will inevitably die at some point, in addition to this, I wanted to confirm that my scepticism about annuity was correct.

How do Life Insurers win against the odds?

As described in our previous chapters, the main difference between life insurance and general insurance is the long-time nature of the life insurance contracts. Life insurance also has short-term products, but most of the products are long term.

Like any other insurance products, life insurance is also based on the principle of pooling many risks in a group and accumulating the funds through the collection of premiums from the customers who are the members of the group. This pool of money is used to pay for the losses of those who die each year (This is somewhat like how the Collegia were operating in Rome – see chapter 1).

For pricing these products, the actuaries project all future cash flows on a probability weighted basis. The projection scenarios are to ensure that the collected premiums and their investment incomes are sufficient to cover the future benefits and expenses but also provide a good return on equity for the insurer.

For each scenario, the actuaries are using several sets of information and assumptions, to name a few: (i) mortality table which will provide the probability of death per age group, (ii) future interest rates and potential investment income, (iii) inflation, (iv) expenses and commissions, (v) volume of policies which will lapse in a given year and finally (vi) provision added to the premium for the insurer's profits.

Life insurance companies are experts in running pricing scenarios to come up with the right premium per insured and ensure that their future liabilities are always sufficiently covered. They translate the risk of dying into a price for coverage (the underwriting part of the process) which also consider the future investment income.

The passage from life into death, which none can avoid, is at the core of life insurance, based on the mortality tables, the actuaries try to estimate when Atropos from the three fates will cut the thread thus determining the individual's moment of death.

Clotho **Lachesis** **Atropos**

What are the sources of income (potential profits) for Life insurers?

Without much surprises, Life insurers share pretty much the same sources of income than P&C insurers: (i) an underwriting income which is the difference between the collected premiums and claims (including expenses) (ii) an investment income from the management of assets that they have accumulated (collected premiums) and finally (iii) a fee income which comes from the fees charged on managing investments on behalf of the policyholders or the insured e.g. 55 basis points (BPS) charged to the assets under management (One basis point is equivalent to 0.01% or 0.0001 in decimal form).

Depending on the products the sources of income will be different, for instance, pure protection products (such as term life insurance) will be heavily dependent on the underwriting profit.

What are the standard life insurance products and their respective business models?

We need to separate the products which have no "savings components" from those which have a savings feature.

Typically, those without savings components are term life policies which cover the risk of death. The benefits are paid only in the event of death, and the policies do not have surrender value (with some exceptions) or a term cash value.

Those with savings components are whole of life, universal life or variable life products. These products combine an insurance protection and a savings feature.

Universal Life credits the policies a rate declared by the insurance company. These policies are long-term contracts with a fixed duration and a fixed face value death benefit plus a surrender value and an end-of-term cash value.

In Europe or Asia, some of the "savings" products are named "unit-linked" products. Those products are equivalent to the "variable universal" life products in the US. For these products as for the Universal Life mentioned earlier, the returns credited to the policies value are based on the performance of the underlying assets. The policies have explicit charges for expenses and cost of insurance which are deducted regularly from the account value.

One could see these policies equivalent to bank savings accounts with a death cover attached to it, but without the flexibility of a bank account in terms of transactions.

As mentioned with the Universal Life products, some insurance products provide a capital guarantee or a guaranteed annual rate of interest, as well as participation in a share of any surplus profits.

We will cover these products later in this book as these features have interesting consequences in terms of cash flow for an insurance company.

Before moving to the insurance products with a savings component, we will cover the "basic" life insurance products often referred to as the "protection" products.

What is the cash flow for Term Life insurance products with a level premium (referred to protection products)?

Term life insurance products have periodic fixed premiums payments over the life of the contract. The payment of commissions and expenses take place in the first year, often exceeding the premium income and therefore creating a negative cash flows. These products typically breakeven after five years when the total premium income exceeds the total expenses from previous years.

Illustration 31: Term life insurance cash flow

The positive net cash flow after the first year is used to generate an investment income. Over time, the premium incomes decline as the policyholders die or the policies lapse. While the collected premium decline, the claims payments are increasing due to higher mortality rates as the insured get older. In the late years of the portfolio, the cash flow turns negative as death benefits overtake the collected premium and the investment income.

Some people say that life insurers are earning their profits with term life products thanks to the high lapse ratio (The lapse ratio represents the percentage of policies that stopped and thus have lapsed in coverage. Typically, an insurance policy will lapse if the policyholder does not pay the premiums). We can find numerous references (accurate or not) to statistics claiming that less than 5% of term policies ever result in a death claim. Is this correct? What are the economic drivers for ensuring that the term life insurance portfolio remains profitable?

How are term life insurance products priced and furthermore why are Insurers able to make a profit with such products?

We will use a simplified example to show how the products are priced.

****

Example 4: Amy's Term Life insurance with InsuR

Amy, 35 years old, is worried for her kids and contacted her InsuR insurance agent for finding an affordable solution to protect her family if she was to pass away. After a long discussion, they agreed to put in place a "term life insurance with guaranteed level premium". She buys a $500,000 policy from Insur to cover her risk of death until she retires at 65 years old.

Since Amy does not smoke and has a healthy life (no use of medicaments and good history), the constant monthly premium is around $50.

Over the next 30 years, under the assumption that Amy pays her premium on time, her family will be protected. If we do the math, we would see that over the lifetime of her policy, Amy would pay a total of $18,000 (30 years x 12 months x $50).

However, this total amount is not what Insur will use for covering Amy's risk of death. If the total premium paid the first year is used to pay the agent's commission and 2% of collected premium used to pay Insur's expenses, the insurance company would get a total of $17,040 to cover the risk.

Total premium paid over 30 years: $18,000

Commission paid the first year: $600 (12 months x $50)

Total Expenses: $360 ($18,000 x 2%)

Total cash to cover the risk: $17,040 ($18,000 - $600 - $360)

The collected amounts are not necessarily what InsuR could use for covering Amy's risk when we include a compound interest of 5% resulting from the investment income (see the illustration 32 below), to simplify the calculation, we are assuming that the 5% gain only applies to the opening balance in any given year (regardless of having a monthly payment).

Illustration 32: Premium Accumulation with a 5% compound interest

Year	Opening balance	Collected premium	Insur's Expenses Commissions	Interest (@ 5%)	Closing Balance
1	$0	$600	-$612.0	$0.0	-$12.0
2	-$12.0	$600	-$12.0	$0.0	$576.0
3	$576.0	$600	-$12.0	$28.8	$1,192.8
4	$1,192.8	$600	-$12.0	$59.6	$1,840.4
...	...	...	...	...	...
27	$28,024.8	$600	-$12.0	$1,401.2	$30,014.1
28	$30,014.1	$600	-$12.0	$1,500.7	$32,102.8
29	$32,102.8	$600	-$12.0	$1,605.1	$34,295.9
30	$34,295.9	$600	-$12.0	$1,714.8	$36,598.7
Total		**18,000**	**$960**	**$19,558.7**	**$36,598.7**

In thirty years, if Amy pays all the premium (which means no death), Insur would collect a total of $18,000 of which $960 would be used to pay internal expenses and commissions but would generate a total profit of $36,598.7 for this policy under the assumption that this amount is not used to pay other claims.

But if Amy unfortunately dies at 40, Insur would have a big loss if she is their unique customer, thus the need to consider the effects of pooling for term life insurance.

****

Even if Insur manages to cover 100,000 customers, how do we know if a $600 yearly premium is enough to cover Amy's risk?

Before getting into the logical process to get to a premium, we need to warn you. Many people view the actuarial field as technical, complicated and, potentially boring. We will try to explain the concepts and basics, but we won't be able to avoid having some "nice formulas".

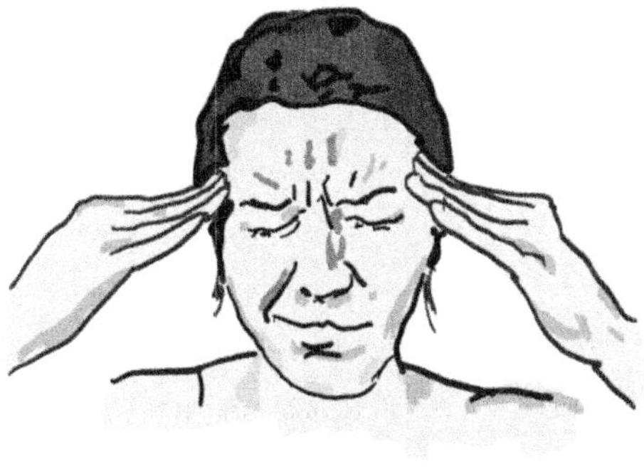

First, we need to cover the concept of Present value (PV) which is the current value of a future sum of money or stream of cash flows given a specified rate of return (interest rate).

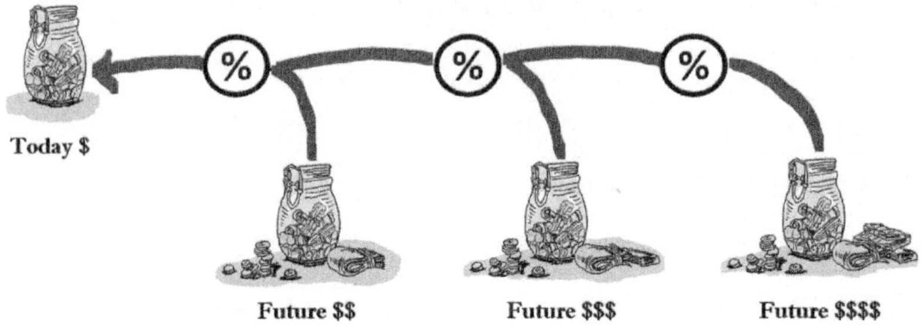

For instance, let's assume that today (at present) you are investing \$1,000 @ 5%. In a year time, this investment will have a value of \$1,050, and in two years, the value will be \$1,102.5.

So, the \$1,050 next year, have a present value of \$1,000.
The \$1,102.5 in two years have a present value of \$1,000.

$\$1,000 = \$1,102.5 / (1 + 5\%)^2$

The formula is at follow:
$PV = FV / (1+r)^n$

PV is Present Value, FV is Future Value, r is the interest rate, and n is the number of years.

Why did we have to introduce the concept of Present Value?

The premium for a term life insurance is from a customer's perspective to cover the risk of death, but from an insurer's perspective, it represents the likelihood of having to pay a death benefit to the beneficiaries.

Therefore, the insurance premium needs to reflect the promises from the life insurance contract. It is defined as the present value of the future death benefit.

Checking the prevent value of a sum in the future is like looking out for it from afar

What do we need to do to come up with a term life insurance premium?

We need to consider several items: the mortality rate, the future interest rate and the load for expenses and insurer's margin.

We will illustrate the whole process with our previous example.

****

Example 5: Amy's Term Life insurance premium Fair Value

For a $500,000 cover, Amy is charged a monthly $40 level premium. Following the previous example, we know by now that a level premium means that Amy will pay a constant premium regardless of her age. At 35 years old, she pays a $600 yearly premium which will be the same when she will turn 64 years old for her last payment. If Amy dies before 65 years old (before the 30th anniversary of the policy), the beneficiary (ies) will get a $500,000 payment from Insur (2 beneficiaries would get $250,000 each).

We are assuming that Amy will pay all her premiums until the end of the policy when she turns 65 years old, we will therefore not consider the effect of "lapse". We are also considering that in the case of death, the insurer will pay the benefits at the end of the year.

Our key assumptions are as follow:

- The Premiums are paid at the beginning of the policy year
- The death claims are paid at the end of the policy year
- The death rate is uniform throughout the year

Activity 1: Estimate the value of the future insurer's payment based on its likelihood in one year

We need to come up with the expected present value of this uncertain payment for the insurer, thus following the below steps

1) In our example, the future death benefit is \$500,000
2) The discount factor is 1/1.05 = 0.952381 if a payment was to be made in a year time (meaning Amy died within a year) – This will provide us with the value of the \$500,000 in a year from now.
3) As per the 2001 female CSO table, 955 out of 984,911 females aged 35 will die within a year. Thus, the probability of Amy to die within a year is 955 / 984,911 = 0.097%.
4) The expected present value of this uncertain payment is (\$500,000) × (.952381) × (0.0009696) = \$461.7

Having achieved this, we need to do the same for the following years.

Activity 2: Follow an iterative approach to compute the PV for the following years

Before coming up with the level premium, we will first calculate the single net premium for Amy's 30 years term policy (from 35 years old to 64 years old).

The 30 years term policy has 30 uncertain future payments. We can calculate these payments as we did for the first year for Amy, this is done with the help of a mortality table (See the illustration 33 on the following page)

Illustration 33: 2001 CSO Mortality Table used in the United States

Age	Females	# dying	Age	Females	# dying
35	984,911	955	51	958,140	3,267
36	983,956	1,014	52	954,873	3,619
37	982,942	1,091	53	951,254	3,995
38	981,851	1,149	54	947,259	4,386
39	980,702	1,206	55	942,873	4,808
40	979,496	1,273	56	938,065	5,282
41	978,223	1,350	57	932,783	5,774
42	976,873	1,446	58	927,009	6,303
43	975,427	1,551	59	920,706	6,804
44	973,876	1,675	60	913,902	7,321
45	972,201	1,818	61	906,581	7,869
46	970,383	1,989	62	898,712	8,439
47	968,394	2,199	63	890,273	9,027
48	966,195	2,415	64	881,246	9,659
49	963,780	2,679	65	871,587	10,328
50	961,101	2,961			

The single net premium for Amy's term life insurance will be the sum of these 30 present values.

As noticed earlier, the CSO mortality table provides us with the likelihood of Amy to die at the age x.

We can quickly come up for every year with the Present Value of the possible payment and Amy's death likelihood (See the illustration 34 on the next page). The single premium net will be the sum of all the net premium, and equal to $21,862.4.

Illustration 34: Single net premium based on the 2001 CSO Mortality table

Age	Amount of Insurance		Probability of death		Present Value of $1 at 5%		Cost of insurance
35	$500,000	X	$\frac{955}{984,911}$	X	0.9524$	=	$461.7 (year 1)
36	$500,000	X	$\frac{1,014}{984,911}$	X	0.9070$	=	$467.4 (year 2)
37	$500,000	X	$\frac{1,091}{984,911}$	X	0.8638$	=	$479.4 (year 3)
...	...		...		...		...
62	$500,000	X	$\frac{8,439}{984,911}$	X	0.2099$	=	$1,092.9 (year 28)
63	$500,000	X	$\frac{9,027}{984,911}$	X	0.1999$	=	$1,113.3 (year 29)
64	$500,000	X	$\frac{9,659}{984,911}$	X	0.1904$	=	$1,134.6 (year 30)
					TOTAL PREMIUM	=	**$21,862.4**

Activity 3: Estimate the PV of a life annuity due of $1

The net annual level premium (NALP) is determined by dividing the net single premium (NSP) by the present value of a life annuity due (PVLAD) of $1 for the premium paying period, which is 30 years.

$$\text{NALP} = \frac{\textbf{NSP (Net single premium)}}{\textbf{PVLAD of \$1 for the premium (paying period)}}$$

The present value of a 30-year term annuity due of $1.0 for a 35 years old woman is, equal to $16.69 (See the illustration 33 on the next page showing the necessary calculation).

Illustration 35: Present value of a life annuity due

Age	% to receive the payment		Present Value of $1 at 5%		Present Value of the Annuity
35			$1 due immediately		
36	$\frac{983,956}{984,911}$	X	0.9070$	=	$0.95 (year 2)
37	$\frac{982,942}{984,911}$	X	0.8638$	=	$0.91 (year 3)
...	...		...		...
62	$\frac{898,712}{984,911}$	X	0.2099$	=	$0.24 (year 33)
63	$\frac{890,273}{984,911}$	X	0.1999$	=	$0.23 (year 34)
64	$\frac{881,246}{984,911}$	X	0.1904$	=	$0.22 (year 35)
			TOTAL PVLAD	=	**$15.78**

To estimate the 30-level annual term life premiums payable at age 35 for a woman, we divide $21,862.4 by $16.69 which is: $21,862.4 / $16.69 = $1309.9 this represents the pure risk premium. We need to add to this the insurer's expenses.

We will assume a loading ratio of 15% (5% for expenses (E) + 10% for profit (Q)).

The gross premium would then be calculated as follow:
G = ($1309.9) / (1 - 0.15) = $1,541

****

In our example 4, we stated that Amy would pay a $50 monthly level premium ($600 per year) which is much lower than our estimates.

How could we explain such a difference between what we found with the CSO mortality table and what insurers are potentially offering?

As described in our example 5, the main drivers for estimating the insurance premium are the mortality table and the discount rate. It is well known that larger insurance companies use their own mortality experience to price their products. The CSO mortality rates are primarily used for reserves and cash values.

In addition, the period life table that we are using, describes the mortality pattern in the population and represents the prospects of longevity for a person when nothing is known about his/her characteristics.

We all know that the life length of a person is a function of several factors such as his/her occupation (truck drivers, slaters have higher accident rates than car mechanics), leisure activities (skydiving might be fun but is more dangerous than cycling), nutrition, smoking and drinking habits.

We can easily find the differences of price between different classes of risks (see illustration 36 on the next page) with "preferred policies" seen as presenting an excellent risk from an insurance perspective (Excellent health and non-smoking customers) to higher risks to be covered for standard policies (Smokers).

Illustration 36: 30-year term life insurance premium per risk class

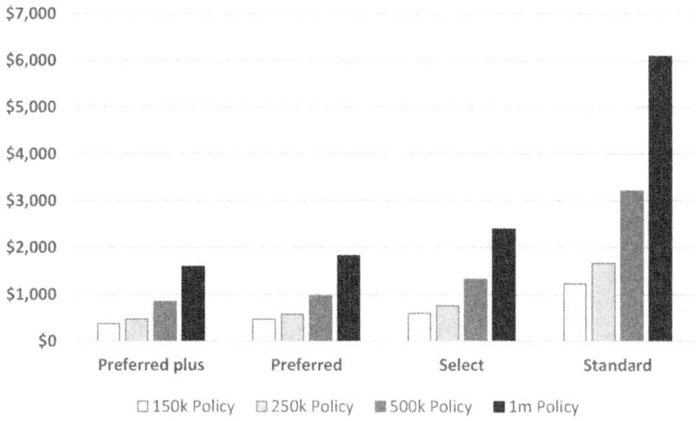

Source Data sourced from TIAA-CREF. Average life insurance illustrations were calculated by looking at four policy amounts ($100k, $250k, $500k, and $1 million) across four Rate Classes.

Slicing and dicing the term life insurance pricing

We know that the main influencing factor on life insurance price is the health of the individual being insured. Information which relate to the smoking habit of an insured, his/her height-to-weight ratio are keys to come up with the annual life insurance premiums. Insured who smoke often pay three times the amount that similar non-smokers will have to pay.

It is understood that the longer the policy term, the more expensive it is for the insured. The average premium cost will be higher as the insured gets older.

As illustrated earlier, to come up with a level premium (the "equivalent" of an "average" premium), the insurers are taking into consideration the changing risks as well as the time value of money (present value and future value) over the period.

At the early stage of the period, the level premium will be much higher than what should be charged for the first years and will become much lower than what would be a premium charged at a later stage of the policy (See illustration 37 below).

As a result, the insurer is building up a liability to the policyholder since the "excess premium" will be used at a later stage to fund the cover. We could see this as an equivalent to the float described earlier. When the policyholder stops paying its premium, thus ending his/her death cover, the insurer is earning the "excess premium".

Illustration 37: Annual Renewable Term life insurance (ART) vs Level term life insurance

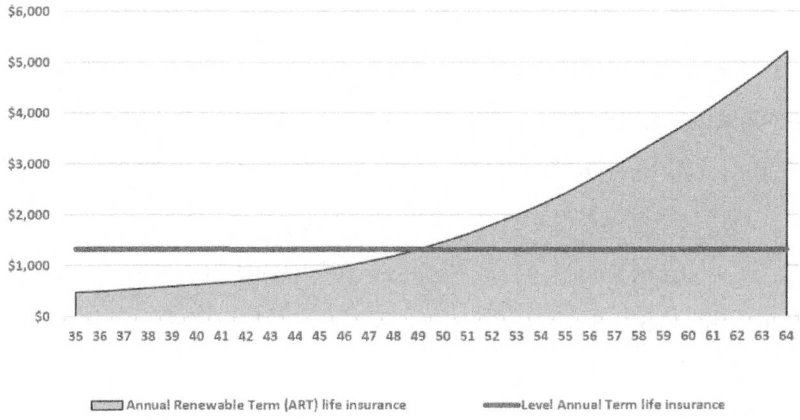

It is also worth noticing that an improvement of life expectancy has a direct impact on the profitability of a term life insurance portfolio. If the policyholders live longer than the estimates from the mortality table (e.g. lower likelihood of death than expected), the death claims are deferred by several years thus improving the profitability of the portfolio (fewer people to die within the policy timeframe). In 2016, the World Health Organisation published a report showing that the Global life expectancy has increased by five years since 2000 which is the fastest increase since the 1960s.

Illustration 38: Rising life expectancy around the world (Source WHO)

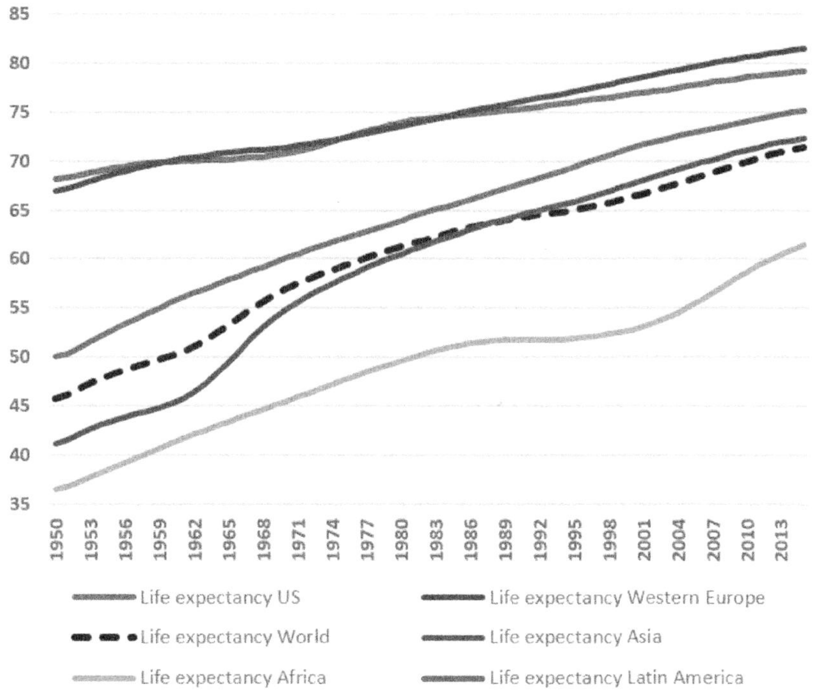

Unforeseen events could have a negative impact to a portfolio, e.g. the recent Opioid Crisis in North America or with another scale, a severe influenza pandemic equivalent to the 1918 Spanish flue which resulted in the death of up to 100 million people worldwide (equivalent to a death toll today of half a billion!). The impact of a pandemic could be severe for life insurers, depending on the insurance portfolio. Increased mortality could cause losses for which the insurers may not be sufficiently prepared.

In a balanced portfolio (annuity, savings and protection products) with a pandemic, one could expect that a "natural hedge" between a rush of life insurance claims and the end of annuity payments would take place. However, this is not always the case, with the Spanish flu in 1918, most of the dead were healthy young adults age 18 to 45. Therefore, a natural hedge did not take place.

Weather events or natural disasters resulting in a significant mortality increase could also have unforeseen consequences to a life insurance portfolio. In a study published in 2001 for the Netherlands, the professors Huynen and Matens observed that heat waves generate a significant increase in mortality among those greater and equal to 65 years of age. Average total excess mortality during the heat waves studied was 12.1% or 39.8 deaths/day.

Their study was rather premonitory when looking at the 2003 heatwave which took place in Western Europe. For instance, in the UK, 102 excess deaths per heatwave day were recorded.

In France, from the 1st of August to the 20th of August 2003, the worst increase took place with roughly 13,500 deaths among the population above 65 years old (675 excess deaths per heatwave day).

For the insurers, the management of the mortality risk is essential.

It is crucial for them to get a large # of insured to mitigate the unsystematic mortality risk which is the risk associated with the randomness of deaths.

However, the systematic mortality risk, which refers to the risk associated with changes in the mortality intensity (or the mortality table) cannot be eliminated nor diversifiable. The consequences of the heat wave in 2003 was a systematic risk.

However, for the systematic mortality risk, a natural hedge could be followed with having portfolios of annuity and protection products.

What is the impact of the expected future interest rate on the premium? And the insurers' profits?

As we have seen in our previous examples, the premium charged to the client is based on assumptions for future interest rates. Like the non-life insurance, life insurers are also expecting to earn an investment income on the premiums paid in advance.

We have run our fair value premium model (described in example 5) with different interest rates (see the illustration 39 below). As expected, we can see a symbiotic relationship between these two, with the insurance premium increasing with lower interest rate and vice versa.

Illustration 39: 30-year term life insurance premium with a different interest rate

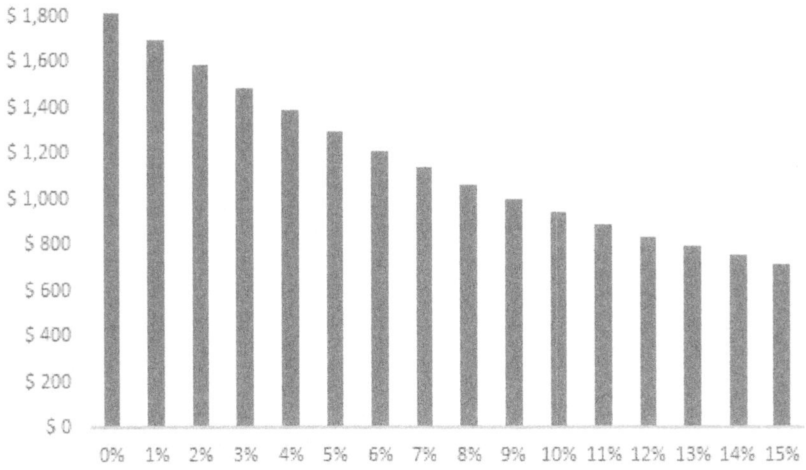

As already described in our previous chapters, insurance is primarily a liability-driven business with the need for insurers to purchase the right assets to match their estimated future insurance obligations (their obligations to pay the future claims covered under the terms and conditions of their products).

Life insurers have much longer liability durations than P&C insurers which have short term liabilities (except for some long tail business lines, see the example of CBL insurance in chapter 3). P&C insurers are mainly managing their short-term needs in terms of liquidity (e.g. short-term investments which can be easily converted into cash to pay the claims).

An increase or decrease of the interest rate has a direct effect on the future insurers' obligations (liability). The changes to the value of this liability are taken through the profit and loss account of the insurer. An increase of the liability is an expense and a decrease of the liability is a profit. Thus, the need for life insurers to ensure that their pricing assumptions are realised and that the collected premiums are invested in assets which provide the specified yield (We will cover this further in chapter eight).

Accurate matching of assets against liabilities is essential to ensure an appropriate allocation of the insurers' investment income against their products to check their profitability.

San Francisco, January 2000

The matching of assets and liabilities is the technique by which the insurers ensure that the life insurance liabilities, from a cash flow perspective, are matched by the appropriate type of assets. In other words, the matching programme provides that when the liabilities are due for payment, there is enough cash available on the asset side. We can observe that life insurers are mainly investing in long term assets such as treasury bond which last for more than ten years (e.g. up to twenty years in Germany).

With regards to the cash flow characteristics (the cash-out in our illustration 31) and the necessary investments to match the future needs, the actuaries will consider the mortality rate but also the lapse ratio for a given portfolio of policies.

We have covered the main economic drivers for the profitability of term life insurance (mortality and returns on investments) but have yet to cover the lapse ratio.

What is the impact of the lapse rate on a portfolio of term life insurance?

Pricing actuaries are aware that they need to have their lapse rate assumption correct to secure the profitability of their portfolio. Lower than expected lapse rates could have a negative impact and impact the insurer's liquidity position.

In Europe, Solvency II (mentioned in chapter 3) introduced the lapse risk valuation in the Standard Formula for estimating the Solvency Capital Requirement (SCR) as well as in internal models. In this framework, the lapse risk refers to "the risk of loss, or of adverse change in the value of insurance liabilities, resulting from changes in the level or volatility of the rates of policy lapses, terminations, renewals and surrenders".

As for getting the right discount rate, it is crucial for insurers to get their lapse ratio right, which is not an easy task. They can base their models on experience but may miss other influencing factors such as the evolving macro-economy conditions and the customers' behaviour.

In a time of recession, customers may stop to pay their term-life insurance premium to realise savings this could result in a higher than expected lapse ratio (which could be positive for an insurer depending of the timing) alternatively when an economy is "booming" the lapse ratio could be lower than average (currently the lowest rates in the US, in two decades at roughly 6% per annum).

To illustrate the "benefits" of lapsing policies, we will use examples 4 and 5. Instead of one customer buying a 30 years level term life policy, we will consider a population of 10,000 women aged 35 years purchasing a $500,000 death cover with an annual level premium of $600 to be paid for 30 years.

We are using the 2001 CSO Mortality Table used in the United States (see the illustration 33). We can quickly build a model which simulates the portfolio of policies with the collected premium and death claims payments. We are assuming a 5% yearly interest rate and that no policies will lapse the first year of the plan. The first-year premium is used to pay the sales' commissions, thus generating a loss for the first year.

The model is to provide on a yearly basis: (a) the # of clients paying a premium (b) the collected premium (c) the claims benefits (d) the expenses (2% of premium) (e) the interest earned per year (5%) and finally (f) the total reserve at the end of the year.

We ran our model for a portfolio of policies under the assumption that no customers will stop paying their premium over 30 years, thus having no lapses. With this scenario, there is a peak of value at 45 years old where the total reserve will be roughly $11m, but when the population reach 52 years old, the portfolio encounters its first loss. At the end of the 30 years, the portfolio will have a total loss of roughly $230m (See the Illustration 40 below and the illustration 41 on the next page).

Illustration 40: Performance of the portfolio at a different age – first loss at 52 years old – No lapses

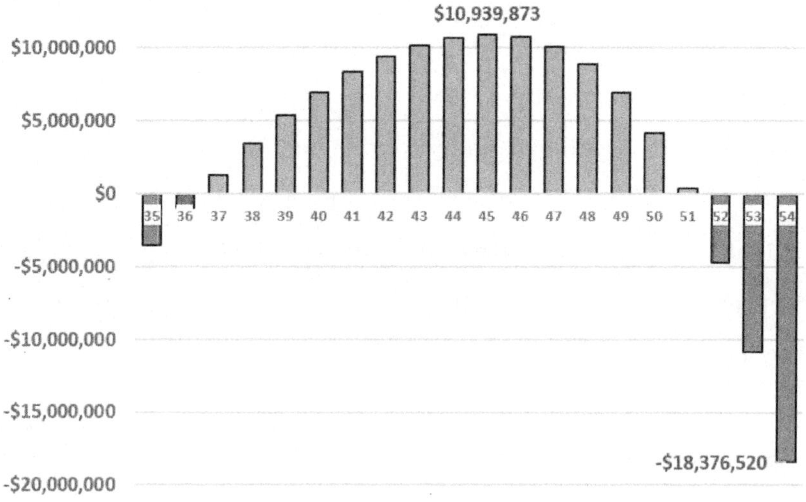

When using different lapse ratio, we can easily see an improvement in the performance of our portfolio with the first year of loss being pushed gradually further. We can observe that the portfolio remains positive throughout the 30 years term when the yearly lapse ratio exceeds 12.5% (under the assumption that no lapse takes place the first year) (see the illustration 41 below).

Illustration 41: Profit of Loss at the end of the 30 years for different yearly lapse ratio.

	Yearly Lapse Rate	Profit or loss at the end of the period	Year of first loss	% of claims paid out
I	0%	-$198m	18	7.50%
II	5%	-$54m	20	3.00%
III	10%	-$9m	25	1.50%
IV	12.5%	$1.3m	No losses	1.10%
V	15%	$7,0m	No losses	0.84%

One could wonder if a yearly lapse rate of 12.5% is a realistic assumption, but you can easily find statistics showing that roughly two-thirds of the policies have lapsed after five years. The critical challenge for the insurers is to have a low lapse ratio in the first years to pay back their initial investment but also to build the necessary reserve for the future cash-out (see the illustration 29).

Often, people will hear statistics that less than 1% of term life insurance policies ever pay a claim, we stated earlier in this chapter a 5% rate. When looking at the CSO table, 757 out of our initial 10,000 women aged 35, will die over the 30 years which is roughly 7.6%, not so far from the 5%.

We could argue that having a good understanding of how much policies will lapse over time makes it possible for insurers to reduce their premium below the pure risk premium, e.g. in our example 5 we found a pure risk premium of $1,300 per year whereas the market is driving the premium below $600.

We used a "basic life insurance" product to illustrate the key profit drivers of a life insurance portfolio, and there are obvious similarities with the non-life insurance products. Life insurers are also generating profits through their insurance operations (Underwriting) and investment operations (Investment results but also fee income). The profitability for protection products such as term life insurance relies on underwriting experience (Mortality risk and lapse ratio) and to a lesser extent also on investment returns. Managing the "pot" (the collected premium) could also be a service to the community of insured.

In our next chapter, we will cover the other spectrum of life insurance, the savings products where the profitability comes mainly from fee income and the investment returns.

CHAPTER 6

THE SAVINGS PRODUCTS

How do insurers sell these products?
What are the sources of revenues for insurers?
What to learn from recent savings scandals?

BY ERIC LEFEBVRE

Chapter Six

No pains, no gains

"There are worse things in life than death. Have you ever spent an evening with an insurance salesman?"
– Woody Allen

Isn't the stock market a casino? France, spring 1999

I am getting ready to move to a new position within the group and trying to finalise some of my last leads. The assistant from our agency in Melun asked me to meet one of our clients to discuss a small investment with us. The team in our insurance agency put in place for Mr Martin, a unit-linked insurance plan with a rather aggressive mix of investments (70% equity, 30% government bonds).

I met our client in a meeting room at our HQ in Paris La Défense, after having him a coffee we went directly to his contracts with us. I had prepared all the necessary documents and had a good view of his investments' performance.

We had a rather thoughtful discussion, but I realised very quickly that he was only interested in the details of the investments, e.g. what was the equity fund invested in? Did they invest in French listed companies such as Air Liquide or Vivendi?

Frankly speaking, the marketing materials that I had on hand, were not very helpful. Yes, Air Liquide was listed, so was Vivendi but I did not have a clue of the volume of these investments? Nor did I know what the fund strategy was.

Mr Martin was rather polite and started explaining to me that he was invested a lot in the stock market. To such a point, that he was thinking of stopping his current activities (he was an employee of Total) and focus exclusively on managing his portfolio.

We continued our exchange and after a while, I got somehow tired of his questions and furthermore lessons. I ended by asking what did he want from our investment plan?

If this was about trading on the stock market, then the plan was not for him. If it was about transferring his wealth to his kids without any inheritance taxes, then the plan was an interesting product.

Of course, the performance of the underneath funds could not match what he was able to achieve with his portfolio which was invested in rather risky assets (we were in the middle of the internet bubble).

Our unit linked insurance plan was clearly not what he needed and he noted that the administration fees were rather high. I offered him instead to put in place a term life insurance which would protect his family while he could invest and follow his own strategy … Of course, he would have to pay income taxes on his earnings, but if his performance was far higher than our annual 9% then it could make sense. Mr Martin appreciated my views and offer, we finally put in place the term life cover, and he surrendered his unit-linked insurance plan.

When the bubble crashed in March 2000, I had some thoughts about Mr Martin and hoped that prior to the crash, he managed to diversify his assets. Thinking about this story, I was wondering if investing in the stock market was the equivalent of gambling in a casino.

It took me several years to wonder if the savings products offered by life insurers, were really an efficient way for the customers to prepare their retirement and/or transfer assets to their children …

This is exactly what we will cover in this chapter. What are the savings products offered by life insurance companies? How do they work and what do they bring to the firms in terms of profit?

But let's start with some thoughts … In most countries, people must have a bank account to receive their pay check but also to pay their rent or pay their income taxes, although it is possible to pay it with hard coins. We may decide to stuff our money between layers of clothes in our wardrobe our below our mattress but one must admit that this is rather inconvenient … not to mention the risk of losing it all as part of a burglary or worst a fire (which is a rather remote risk).

Buying a brand-new car in cash could also be challenging as we would have to carry loads of money in our wallet. Nowadays, it is getting difficult (if not impossible) to pay with very large notes.

One reason being that central banks are slowly but surely removing the big notes. For instance, in 2016, the European Central announced that it would stop issuing the so-called "Bin Laden banknote" or 500-euro banknote, claiming the usual palaver about fighting "money laundering" and furthermore "financing terrorism". The same trend is happening in other Western countries, with officials asking to scrap high-denomination banknotes such as the $100, CHF1'000 and £50 notes.

Transferring cash to people is also rather difficult, of course we can send money and pay bills via wire transfer from services like Western Union for a fee or Xe Money Transfer.

Without a bank account, borrowing money is almost impossible. We can find some "nice" lenders which will offer small loans but the interest rates and fees could be very high.

As mentioned earlier, having all our savings in our house would expose us to the risk of losing it totally in case of fire or burglary. Whereas, in theory, our savings are safe when placed in a bank account which is under a depositor protection scheme with country specific limits e.g. in the US, the standard deposit insurance coverage limit is $250,000 per depositor, per FDIC-insured bank, per ownership category.

Finally, as described in our previous chapter, the time value of money tells us that a dollar today is worth more than a dollar tomorrow. This means that the value of the money kept below our mattress will decline over time. However, if we manage to invest this money and gain a good rate of return, we might be able to keep up with inflation and/or exceed it

The only advantage (so to speak) when keeping our "savings" below our mattress is to be able to transfer it to our loved ones without having them to pay any taxes. There is one major issue, in case of death: there is no way we could ensure that our heirs will receive our savings. Having said this, in case of death, in most cases, the bank accounts are off limits for the heirs until everything is settled in court (except for joint accounts and/or trusts).

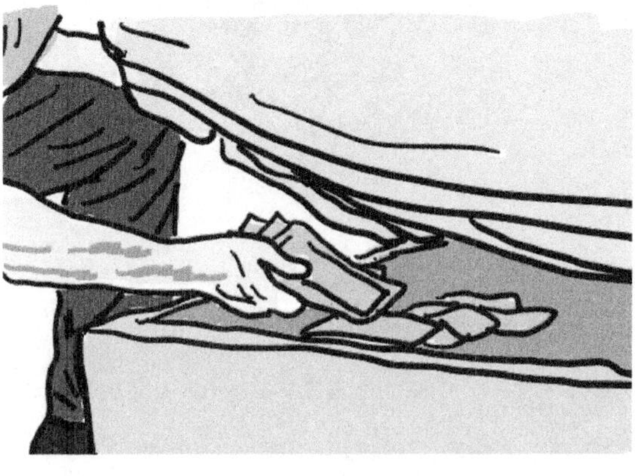

Clearly having a bank account has numerous advantages such as paying our bills, financing the purchase of a house but also making our money working. There is a major drawback though: In case of death, the transfer of our savings to our loved ones will not take place automatically and are taxable.

How could we resolve this problem without having to keep a substantial amount of cash below our mattress?
This is where some insurance products are bringing an interesting advantage: In most cases, life insurance death proceeds are not taxable to the beneficiary. With this, life insurance products are clearly protecting our family. Unfortunately, life insurers still must make some progress in paying swiftly the death claims benefits to the designated beneficiaries.

The term life products (introduced in our previous chapter) are standard and do not have a cash value. With these products, the only cash value is to the beneficiaries who will receive the "non-taxable" death benefit.

The life insurance products with a cash value provide both death benefits and savings features. It is the equivalent of a savings account wrapped with a death cover. When an insured buys a cash value policy, part of his/her premium pays for the life insurance protection and part of his/her premium goes to the savings account. The savings portion of the premiums are invested, the "principal" and "earned interests" accumulate over time as the cash value of the policy.

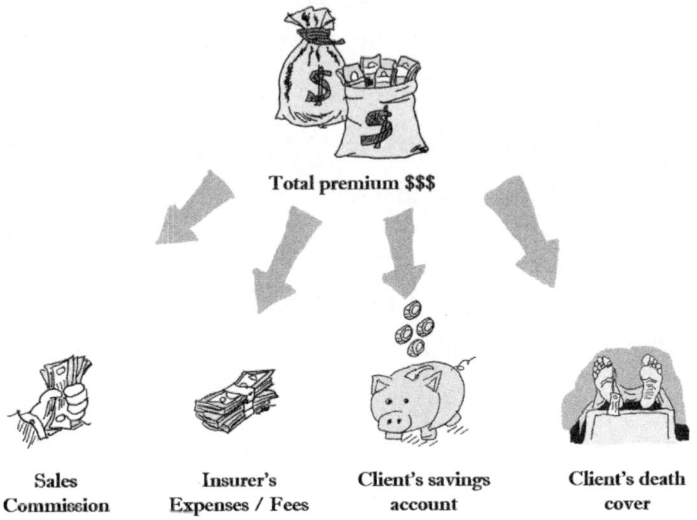

Recently, I reviewed an endowment plan of a friend. The whole story started when we discussed the products sold in Germany with a guaranteed rate of return. He mentioned that he bought one of these great investment plans back in 2003 and was very pleased with receiving a 3.7% guaranteed rate of return on a policy without any risk.

I had to admit that this seemed very encouraging and very difficult to find these days ... and yet I challenged him by asking some questions: Which part of the paid premium was effectively invested? Has he ever checked the rate of return displayed on his yearly statement? Will his wife or kids receive a lump sum for his death on top of his savings plan? We will discuss the results of the review at the end of this chapter, having said that, this discussion brings us to the following questions:

Why would customers want such "savings" products? How do Insurers attract their customers?

Putting aside the "protection features", the "savings products" are not dissimilar to the investment opportunities offered by the banks.

With their cash value accumulation, these products are sold to help the "insured" to meet their future financial needs such as funding their future retirement, childrens' studies or purchasing a property. Therefore, combining a "term life insurance" with a savings account, allows the insured to protect their family (in case of death, ensuring that their loved ones still get an income) and to finance future expenses at a given date.

The insurance companies are designing their insurance savings plans also called endowment plans, to help their clients to achieve long term saving goals.

But the protection aspects are clearly not the main selling point, as mentioned earlier, in case of death, the benefits are not "taxable" but there are also other tax advantages for the policyholder with these endowment plans. Some of the opportunities to optimise the policyholder's taxes could be significant.

In many countries, the government give a tax-advantaged status to encourage people to fund their future retirement and/or to a certain extent, fund the purchase of a house. For instance, in some countries, the contributions to these plans (up to a certain limit) could be deducted from the policyholder's taxable income (See the example 7 on the next page).

****

Example 7: Amy's Tax Situation

Let's assume that Amy is living in a country where she could deduct from her taxable income a contribution to an endowment plan of up to $7,000 per year. Depending on her income and highest tranche (see the illustration 42 below), her benefits will range from roughly $2,000 to $2,800 per year, a rather good incentive

Illustration 42: Income Tax Brackets

Single	Tax rate	Savings in full
$91,150 to $190,150	28%	$1,960
$190,150 to $413,350	33%	$2,310
$413,350 to $415,050	35%	$2,450
$415,050 or more	39.60%	$2,772

****

There could be additional tax arbitrage opportunities for Amy. Depending on the country, the investment gains generated within the policy are tax-deferred and will only be taxed when Amy takes the gains out of her policy through withdrawals or surrenders.

If Amy was living in the UK and took her endowment life policy there, her gains at maturity would not be taxable when the product fulfils certain conditions e.g. a premium payment term of at least 10 years, a broadly even spread of premiums (payable at least once a year) and the capital sum payable on death must be at least 75% of the total premiums payable over the whole term.

Finally, the insurers are also promoting the opportunity to grow the policyholders' investments within the plans. To achieve this, there are different options (products) offered to customers with the possibility to have a guaranteed rate of return (generally rather low). It is worth noting that products with guaranteed rate of return are not offered in all countries.

Illustration 43: Proportion of the life insurance contracts with guaranteed returns in Germany

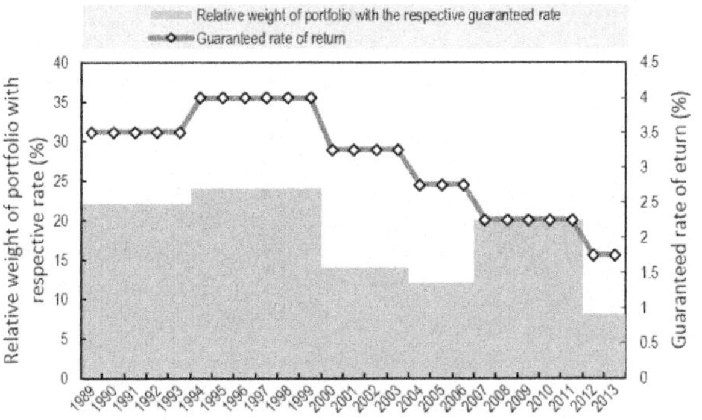

Source: Based on estimates from Berdin and Gründl (2014).

With some products, the insurer is entirely in charge of the allocation of the assets which will be a mix of equity and fixed-income investments. The clients do not have that much control over the underlying investments. This is the product that my friend bought in 2003 with a guaranteed rate of return which means that the insurer supports the investment risk.

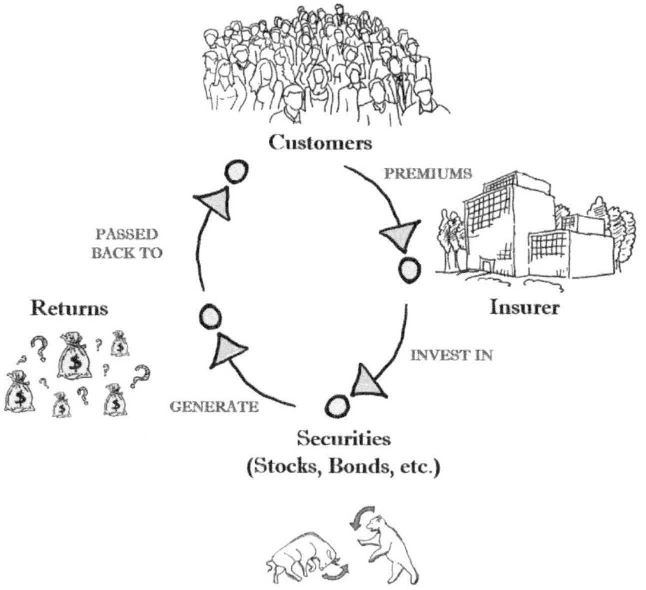

Alternatively, the clients can choose products which offer them to invest on a unit-linked basis. With these, they have access to a range of different investment funds which are either run by the insurance company or collective investment scheme (CIS) ran by other firms such as open-ended investment companies (OEICs). At any time, the customers have the option to invest / switch between the different funds (debt or equity) or a mix of both based on their investment need and appetite. These products provide clients with some "flexibility" to manage their investments.

How do unit-linked policies work? What are the sources of revenues for the insurers?

Part of the customers' premiums are pooled together and used to buy units in one or several unit-linked funds. The customers can choose the funds for their investment based on their risk appetite. These funds invest in a wide range of assets, for instance, the "InsuR North American Shares Fund" would invest exclusively in shares traded in the United States.

The customers do not have any leverage on the investment decisions, other than switching their cash to another fund and/or surrender their policy "usually" with a significant cost. The investment manager decides the mix of assets in a fund based on investment guidelines, thus a very "limited" investment flexibility for the customers. The customers do not have that much freedom, their policy becoming the equivalent of the grill in a jail.

Each fund (and/or pool) is divided into units, which represents an equal share of the fund. When a customer selects a fund for his/her investment, he/she buys some units in the fund. On the contrary, when he/she switches to another fund, he/she sells some of his/her units back to the insurer before investing in the new fund. The units are bought at an offer price but are often worth only a lower bid price. The insurer earns the bid-offer spread on each unit purchased, we will illustrate this concept with the below example.

****

Example 8: Amy's unit-linked policy with Insur

Amy decides to apply for a unit-linked life insurance policy with Insur. In the application, she asks to invest her premium in several funds including the "InsuR North American Shares Fund".
How many units will she get when investing $10,000 in this fund?

We are assuming that the fund has a total value of $400,000 with 40,000 units. Therefore, each unit has a price set at $10 ($400,000 divided by 40,000). The value of this unit will go up and down as it reflects the value of the underlying assets and is not guaranteed.
The units won't be offered to Amy at $10 each as InsuR defines on a daily basis bid and offer prices for its funds. We will estimate her that InsuR will sell the unit at $10.24 which is the offer price.

The bid and offer prices are defined as the following:
A bid price – the price used to value the funds when Amy will cash in her units – Bid price set at $9.756
An offer price – the price that represents what Amy will pay when buying the units – Offer price set at $10.24

InsuR is selling to Amy the units at a 5% higher price (the offer price) than what will be paid to a customer who sells the units back to InsuR (the bid price). The difference between the two prices is called the bid-offer spread.

In our example, for $10,000, Amy will receive 976.2 units ($10,000 / $10.24) and her total investment will be valued at $9,524 (976.2 x $9.756).

In other words, she would lose 5% of her initial investment.

****

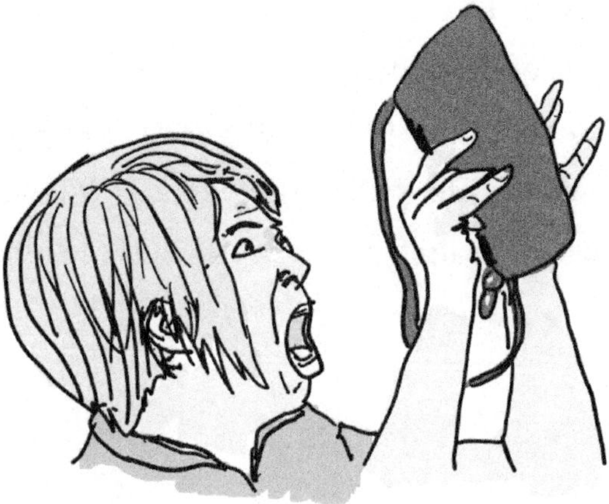

Like any "life insurance product with a cash value", Unit linked insurance plans are combining a death cover with an investment component. But the latest is very similar to what mutual funds would offer to their investors. With these arrangements, the policyholders bear all the investment risks as it is the case with any mutual fund. On top of the mortality charges for the insurance part, the insurers are charging several fees, the bid-offer spread is one of their sources of revenues.

What are the fees collected by the insurers throughout the life of a policy?

It is worth mentioning that this is an area where insurers are usually not very transparent and is a source of problems and issues. With the insurers' practices, it should not come as a surprise that they have the lowest Net Promoter Score (NPS) ratings of any industry.

Are the customers rightly complaining about the portion of the premium which gets effectively invested?
Before reviewing all the costs involved, we need to understand the structure in place for a unit-linked insurance plan and the parties involved. There are four main parties: the insurance broker or agent (the one selling the policy to the customer), the insurance carrier, the asset manager (the one who manages the investments) and the custodian bank (responsible for holding and safeguarding the securities). All these parties have their own costs which will be covered by the customers' premiums throughout the life of the policy.

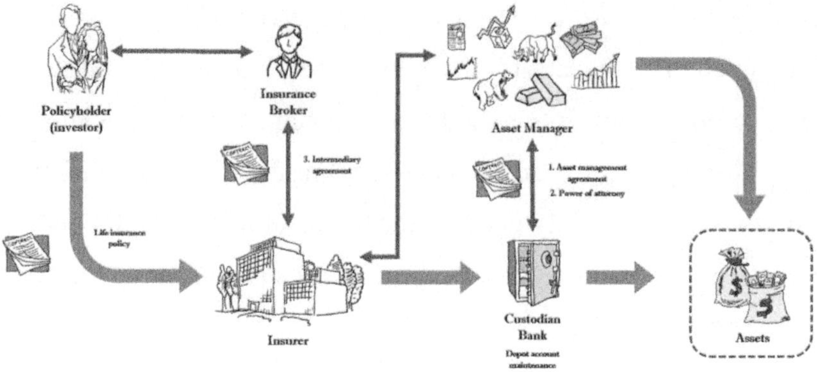

Many customers do not know the total cost of their unit linked insurance plans, partly because the insurers are not very transparent.

The table on the next page provides an overview of the main expenses for each party.

Parties	Fees description	Min % on total assets	Max % on total assets
Insurer	Establishment fee	0.2	1.5
	Yearly fees for administration	0.3	1.5
	Fund switching fees	0	0.4
	Bid/offer spread	5	
	Mortality charge	1% × Sum at risk at the end of the year after fees	
Insurance Broker	Up-front commission	2	5
	Yearly commission	0	0.5
Asset Manager	Annual fee	0.5	2
	Performance fee on returns*	0*	20*
Custodian Bank	Account opening charges	0	0.1
	Depot fees	0.15	0.5
	Transaction fees	0.5	2

*as a percentage of the investment gains

How much of these charges levied impact the overall returns?

We will use an example to show the impacts of these charges to the customers' assets over 10 years and how much the charges levied will take from all returns.

****

Example 9: Charges levied on Amy's unit-linked policy with Insur

We are assuming that Amy is investing $50,000 with a single premium in a unit-linked insurance plan for a 10-year duration. As part of the plan, she requested a death cover of $70,000. Amy is opting for a balanced strategy of 50 percent equity (fund 1), 40 percent bonds (fund 2) and 10 percent in high risk alternative investments (fund 3). For fund 3, a 20% annual performance fee will apply on the gains.

	Raw annual return	Bid Price	Value	Offer price
Equity – Fund 1	8%	$200	$205	$210
Bond – Fund 2	4%	$150	$153.75	$157.5
High Risk – Fund 3	15%	$300	$307.5	$315

The death benefit is $70,000 but the "sum at risk" for Insur is the difference between the death benefit and the assets in the unit-linked funds. The "sum at risk" will decrease over time as the underlying assets grow. We will use the table on the previous page for assessing the impacts on the performance, and run two scenarios: Low and High-end.

At the issuance of the policy, we need to estimate the premium which will be invested in units. We will call this Year 0.

For the scenario 1 (Low-end), we will have the following charges

Brokers' commission: 2% of $50,000 = $1,000

InsuR's establishment fees: 0.2% of $50,000 = $100

InsuR's yearly fees for administration: 0.3% of $50,000 = $150

Asset Manager annual fees: 0.5% of $50,000 = $250

Custodian bank – account opening charges = $0

Custodian bank – depot fees = 0.15% of $50,000 = $75

Total premium to be invested before mortality charges = $48,425

	Premiums to be invested	**Offer Price**	**# of units**	**Value**
Equity – Fund 1 50%	$24,212.5	$210	115.3	$23,636.5
Bond – Fund 2 40%	$19,370	$157.5	123	$18,908.8
High Risk – Fund 3 10%	$4,842.5	$315	15.4	$4,727.2
Total	**$48,425**			**$47,272**

To come up with the mortality charge, we will use the total value of the investment. The "sum at risk" is $70,000 less $47,272 which gives $22,728. The mortality charge is therefore $227 (1% of $22,728). We are simplifying the model by not considering the need to sell units to pay for the mortality charge and a larger "sum at risk" required.

After all charges have been levied, Amy's total investment is $47,045 (a 6% decrease from the initial $50,000).

<u>For the scenario 2 (High-end), we will have the following charges</u>

Brokers' commission: 5% of $50,000 = $2,500

InsuR's establishment fees: 1.5% of $50,000 = $750

InsuR's yearly fees for administration: 1.5% of $50,000 = $750

Asset Manager annual fees: 2% of $50,000 = $1,000

Custodian bank – account opening charges: 0.1% of $50,000 = $50

Custodian bank – depot fees = 0.5% of $50,000 = $250

Total premium to be invested before mortality charges = $44,450

	Premiums to be invested	**Offer Price**	**# of units**	**Value**
Equity – Fund 1 50%	$22,225	$210	105.8	$21,696
Bond – Fund 2 40%	$17,780	$157.5	112.9	$17,357
High Risk – Fund 3 10%	$4,445	$315	14.1	$4,339
Total	**$44,450**			**$43,392**

To come up with the mortality charge, we will use the total value of the investment. The "sum at risk" is $70,000 less $43,392 which gives $26,610. The mortality charge is therefore $266 (1% of $26,610). We are simplifying the model by not considering the need to sell units to pay for the mortality charge and a larger "sum at risk" required.

After all charges have been levied, Amy's total investment is $43,126 (a 13.3% decrease from the initial $50,000). This is already a serious handicap for future performance.

At year 0, Amy's investments would be as follow:

Year 0	Scenario 1	Scenario 2
Equity – Fund 1 50%	$23,522	$21,563
Bond – Fund 2 40%	$18,818	$17,250
High Risk – Fund 3 10%	$4,704	$4,313
Total	**$47,045**	**$43,126**

At year 1, before all the charges, the investments are gaining some returns

Year 1	Rate of return	Scenario 1	Scenario 2
Equity – Fund 1 50%	8%	$25,404	$23,288
Bond – Fund 2 40%	4%	$19,571	$17,940
High Risk – Fund 3 10%	15% (but 20% to be collected for performance)	$5,269	$4,830
Total		**$50,244**	**$46,058**

And we will have the following charges

Charges at the end of Year 1	**Scenario 1**	**Scenario 2**
Insurer yearly fees for administration	$151	$691
Insurance Broker yearly commission	$0	$230
Asset Manager annual fees	$251	$921
Custodian bank depot fees	$75	$230
Total expenses before the mortality charge	$477	$2,072
Mortality charges	$202	$260
Policy value end of Year 1	**$49,564**	**$43,725**

We can easily project the future cash flow for each scenario. Over 10 years, the total costs per scenario for Amy will be as follow:

	Scenario 1	**Scenario 2**
Total levied charges	$9,903	$31,167
Policy cash value at the end of the period	$82,159	$52,714
Annualized rate of return	5.1%	0.5%
Cost as a % of the paid premium ($50,000)	20%	62%

With the worst-case scenario, Amy is getting an annualized rate of return of 0.5% and with the best-case scenario, she gets a 5.1% rate of return. The two scenarios are rather extreme for the insurance industry but give an idea of how these plans work and furthermore what the customers are potentially paying to have their savings managed by "professionals".

****

In our example, we have not mentioned the potential impacts of switching between funds. In 2008, at the top of the financial crisis, some customers discovered the impacts of the bid/offer spread to their portfolio (but also potential administration charges).

As we can see, there are in the market, some "financial products" which are clearly benefitting the product manufacturers (in other words the insurers) and the sales person (the brokers) instead of providing an adequate service to the customers.

Most unit-linked insurance plans do also have surrender charges when the customers decide to withdraw their savings earlier than expected e.g. within the first 3 years, customers may have to pay a rather high charge to surrender.

For information, my friend's "great" German endowment plan has a 10% surrender charge ...

In one market, we found an insurer which offers products where the acquired units during the first 18 months (the initial units) have no value until the 18 months are up. In other words, the surrender value of this unit-linked plan for the initial 18 months period is $0.

All the levied charges are making some unit-linked insurance plan rather expensive for the customers, roughly from 1.5% per year up to 5% (and above) levied from the total assets. The policies are not really designed to be retirement savings accounts and furthermore the death cover is usually more expensive than what a customer could get separately.

In multiple countries, there are growing concerns over the commissions paid to the distributors (banks, brokers, etc.) and customers' discontents with the performance of their investments.

The main problem with the unit-linked insurance plan is that they offer three benefits to the customers: a life cover, tax savings and wealth creation and are rather complex. As a result, the clients may misunderstand the aim of the products and only focus on the wealth creation thus being surprised with poor returns in the early years of the plan.

Over the past decade, several scandals have put nails in the coffin of these "savings plan".

The "Woekerpolis" scandal in the Netherlands found insurers guilty of "milking" their customers by miss-selling millions of unit-linked policies. Many of which were sold based on poor advice that failed to disclose the high fees these policies incurred. The Dutch Authorities discovered that the information provided to the customers before signing a contract, was incomplete, insufficient and sometimes wrong …

It was unclear for the customers that an important part of the sum paid in, was not invested, but covered the (administrative) costs, commission and death cover premium. This combined with declining stock markets caused a very bad return of the investments and disappointing wealth creation for the customers.

The common theme with the "Woekerpolis" scandal is that the customers were not informed how much of their premiums were effectively invested, and how much used to cover the insurers' and other intermediaries' costs (including the commissions to the sales forces).

There is a fundamental flaw in the way the life insurance products are being distributed and/or pushed to the end customers. We started this chapter describing the challenge of handling cash without a bank account and furthermore managing the fruits of one's labour, not to mention transferring it to another generation. All these are the benefits of life insurance products but provide fertile ground to miss-sell them.

Often the consumers do not get the advice they really need and this is in part due to the commissions paid to the distributors and/or the sales incentives provided to the Insurers' sales forces. Putting their financial interests before those of their customers, the sales forces steer the customers towards complex and expensive products which may not be suitable for them. We should all think of the Stock Selling Scene from the movie "The Wolf of Wall Street".

The unit-linked insurance plans are more and more under the regulators' scrutiny. In many countries, new sets of rules are being introduced to protect the consumers and stop up-front payments of commissions to intermediaries.

For instance, in 2014, the Hong Kong's insurance authority banned upfront commission payments on long-term policies in a move to clean up an HK$17 billion-a-year business plagued by persistent complaints from customers. The insurers were paying a claw back to the brokers based on the full value of the policy.

The regulator decided to provide an end to this practice: "Indemnity commission, or any standing arrangement that offers advance payment of a commission, is strictly prohibited. Insurers should only pay commission on an earned basis," said the rules, which was due to come into force on January 1, 2015. "Commission payable should also spread over an appropriate duration to encourage good after-sale service and duly reward long-term relationship between intermediaries and policyholders."

Hong Kong followed the example of the Netherlands where the regulator effectively banned in 2013 the commissions on financial products including protection. The process started in 2006 when the first change to the clawback process was implemented, and gradually forced a change in the adviser cash flow model.

We can only anticipate the end of up-front commissions being paid to the distributors of life insurance. This will provide major challenges to the insurers.

We could argue that high commissions were "motivating" salespeople to distribute unattractive products. With no commissions and/or reduced incentives, the distributors will most likely look at selling other products than insurance which would help them to maintain their income.

When looking at unit-linked insurance or endowment plans, we may wonder why people do not invest directly in several mutual funds and purchase separately a term life insurance cover of the same amount instead of investing in these products.

What does it mean for the future of these products?

The insurers must raise their games, they will have to improve their savings products to get them attractive for the customers or deliver the services that their customers really need.

For attracting new customers and/or cash from existing ones, offering insurance products with "high guarantees" (even any guarantee at all) is no longer an option since the insurer cannot match the future liabilities with bonds which offer adequate yields. In addition, these products are consuming lots of capital holding under the Solvency II regulations (in Europe).

The insurers are left with offering "capital light" products such as unit-linked insurance plans while having to change their incentive models including the commissions paid to the distributors (brokers, agents or banks).

The problem with this approach is that on one hand, these products are rather complex and need to be carefully explained to the customers, and on the other hand the insurers will have difficulties in finding salespeople willing to get trained and to provide an advice to the customers for a very small (if any) commission. This could be a causality dilemma for life insurers.

To resolve their causality dilemma, some insurers have decided to become asset managers and to sell their legacy book of businesses. It is yet to be seen if this is the right strategy, with the next recession to come, we could only wonder how the life insurers will weather the next storm to come, with their customers having to face the paradox of thrift.

The paradox of thrift states that during a recession, people stop spending and tend to save more thus an increase in their planned savings. As a result, the demand for goods decreases and the value of the investment also decreases, in other words the more people save during a recession the more the markets get depressed and the more the value of their investments decreases. This ends up in a downward spiral.

This will not be good for the life insurers who won't be able to provide good returns for their customers (a depressed financial market) plus will face pressure to reduce the costs of their unit linked insurance plans. In addition, we can only anticipate that the governments will do everything to push people to spend and may stop the incentives currently in place for saving such as the tax advantages of the unit linked insurance plans.

I mentioned earlier in this chapter, my friend's endowment policy and its "supposedly" high safe guaranteed rate of return of 3,7%. We will review this one here.

****

What are the facts for the great German endowment plan?

Start date of the plan: 01/01/2003

First yearly premium: 300€

Automatic increase of premium on a yearly basis: 10%

Death cover and payment of the latest premium in case of an accident until the end of the plan

End of the plan: 2042 (when my friend reached 65 years old

Exit of the plan as capital or annuity

Interest rate: 3.7%

For 2018, the insurer mentioned a gain of 4% with the help of the participation gain.

My friend is very happy with this plan. I was already showing lots of doubts and had to find a way to explain nicely the problem.

Sadly, my friend was trusting what the insurer was writing in his annual statement and never checked how much had been paid so far nor how much was put in the savings plan.

The current capital for his plan is roughly 8,000€.

How much has my friend paid so far?
This is rather an easy calculation, since 2003, roughly €10,800 had been paid. Clearly the insurer took much more for the accident and death cover than we were both anticipating, an amount exceeding 2,800€!

We ran a quick estimate and found out that roughly €250 were paid to the insurer for the additional cover and administrative expenses on a yearly basis. Since 2003, 4000€ has been paid to the insurer. By 2042, the total payment to the plan would be roughly 133,000€ and the total capital 178,000€. This is clearly not a great savings plan.

My friend decided to call the insurer, I am wondering if he was louder than an angry German shepherd?

By now, we hopefully managed to cover how the savings products work and what is at the core of the insurers' business model. By now, we should have a good understanding of the "insurance machine" and furthermore their potential Achilles heel (e.g. interest rates, economy and mortality risks).

We have not yet covered the "annuity products" which are also rather interesting as a source of revenues for the insurers. We could argue that these products are what separate the insurers from the banks. This will be covered in a separate chapter in this book.

Earlier in this book, we covered Solvency II and partly introduced the concept of capital requirements for insurers. These requirements are pushing the insurers to distribute "capital light" products but their legacies are still hindering them. Matching the insurers' liabilities with the right investments is key to maintain their solvency and this could be a problem in stressed financial markets.

At the top of the 2008 crisis, we experienced what most people forgot about, the existence of bank run. The type of memory that we thought, was buried in the 1920s and 1930s.

Could such things happen to insurers? Most of us remember AIG and how this iconic financial powerhouse went down but are there other examples which could be useful for those who want to learn about insurance? This will be what we will cover in our next chapters, what are the potential impact of monetary policies to insurers and/or the collapse of financial markets?

CHAPTER 7

THE BIGGEST QUARTERLY LOSS IN CORPORATE HISTORY

How the largest insurer in the world collapsed?
What can we learn from this event?
Could we have anticipated this tragic outcome?

BY ERIC LEFEBVRE

Chapter Seven

Hang on and Enjoy the Ride

"In the ten years since the financial panic, we have learned we are all dominoes spaced closely together"
– Warren Buffett

Who is trustworthy? – Finland, Summer 2008

It had been one year since Eddy and I went to buy a laptop for him. Then daily he came to my place to access internet but also to discuss. He was on vacation in Finland and needed to do some transactions through his brokerage account to weather the crisis. The market correction was in full swing. Early August 2007, France's biggest listed bank, BNP Paribas, froze 1.6 billion euros ($2.2 billion) worth of funds, citing the U.S. subprime mortgage sector woes that rattled financial markets worldwide.

As a result, the markets were crashing, and Eddy was receiving margin calls, he ultimately would lose two apartments and some savings. Eddy did not like my views that this crisis would last four to five years and that further losses were to be expected.

What a year, full of events that only a few fully understood in the middle of this market meltdown, in January 2008, I decided that it was the best time to go around the world. While travelling, in March 2008, I read the news of Bear Stearn going bust. The banks were clearly severely impacted.

On my way back to Europe from California, I decided to stop in New York, to meet some senior executives that I knew in AIG. Our discussion was about my next project with them which would start in August 2008.

When looking at the insurers, I naively thought that they would weather well this financial crisis as they always did with some exceptions. Even if AIG lost their prized AAA rating in 2005, I kept admiring this financial institution and always enjoyed working with their teams.

In August 2008, my contacts at AIG in New York informed me that the start of our project would be pushed to October 2008. I did not see anything wrong with this, although things were really getting crazy in the financial markets with Lehman Brothers on the verge of collapse.

The run on Northern Rock in the UK which took place one year earlier (in September 2007) seemed relatively insignificant when considering a possible collapse of Lehman Brothers. Back then, most depositors in Western countries had no memory of a bank failure. Hearing that in a single day, the Northern Rock's customers pulled out £1bn was truly disturbing, they feared that they would not get in full what was on their account. People did not believe anymore that their bank deposits were safe.

Then on the 15th of September 2008, Lehman Brothers filed for bankruptcy triggering the "great panic" of 2008. On the 16th of September 2008, AIG was rescued by the Federal Reserve from failure with an $85 billion two-year loan.

Due to losses from Lehman's bankruptcy, investors fled money market mutual funds. That's where companies keep their cash. On the 16th of September 2008, the Reserve Primary Fund "broke the buck." It didn't have enough money on hand to pay out all the redemptions that were occurring.

On the 17th of September, the attack spread. Investors withdrew a record $144.5 billion from their money market accounts. During a typical week, only about $7 billion is withdrawn.

By the 2nd of March 2009, AIG reported the largest loss in corporate history. It had lost a record $61.7 billion in the fourth quarter of 2008. Warren Buffet's Berkshire Hathaway posted its largest book loss in its history: reporting $4.99 billion net income, or $3,224 per share, in 2008. That's down from $13.21 billion, or $8,548, in 2007.

With regards to my great project with AIG, it did not take place... As I was contemplating the collapse of the financial market, I realized that I was wrongly assuming that insurers were safer than banks and hardly ever go bankrupt.

I could not be so wrong. Since 2008, I have run some research on this topic and realized that there had been numerous failures of insurers which were not put to the spotlight, except for AIG of course. There are lots of lessons to be learned from these collapses (or near collapses).

We will cover first the AIG case as it provides us with some interesting lessons when looking at the financial performance of an insurer.

How did a boring, supposedly safe insurance company with more than a trillion dollars of assets become the largest bailout in the 2008 financial crisis?

There are lots of articles or books describing how AIG collapsed, we will summarise here the chain of events which put them down as there are lessons to be learned out of these. We will do this with an "insurer's hat".

Over the years, in search for additional revenues and to improve their margins, AIG entered the world of financial engineering by selling Credit Default Swaps (CDS) but also providing Securities lending. For these activities, one of the main selling points for AIG was their coveted "AAA".

The CDS were the main culprit for AIG's problems with a loss exceeding $30 billion, but their securities lending brought additional losses exceeding $21 billion.

What are CDS?

A credit default swap (CDS) is the equivalent of an insurance contract which covers the risk of a debt default. This is very similar to a Trade Credit Insurance which covers the risk that an exporter will not be able to recover his bills from an importer. Wall Street bankers love using complex words (or exotic ones) to describe simple things.

Like any insurance contract, the "insurer" must price the risk (in this case of default) and bill a premium to the buyer. The insurer also must set-up the necessary reserves for future claims.

What happened with those CDS?

Over the years, AIG had become a major seller of credit default swaps through its subsidiary AIG Financial Products Corporation (AIGFP). These swaps were covering the assets that supported corporate debt and mortgages. The outstanding amount of CDS grew rapidly from the late 1990s until 2007 with AIG being a prime actor of this market.

In 2002, under the management of Joseph Cassano, AIGFP started offering the type of credit default swaps (CDS) that got AIG into trouble. It is worth mentioning that AIGFP began to enter derivatives transactions back in 1987.

By the end of 2007, through its swaps, AIG covered about $61 billion in securities with exposure to subprime mortgages. The problem with these securities was that if their prices collapsed, AIG had to fulfil its commitments and unfortunately did not have enough reserve (pretty much the same issue than CBL with its long-tail liabilities discussed in one of our previous chapters).

What went wrong with AIGFP which was for years a cash cow for AIG?

Unfortunately for AIG, the CDS sold by AIGFP had a "double whammy".

First, AIG was forced to pay increasing losses as the value of the securities which were guaranteed by AIG was deteriorating. Since the reserves were not high enough, AIG had to use some of its capital to pay the "insured". This led to a deterioration of AIG financial position thus threatening its credit rating with dire consequences under the CDS agreements.

Second, under the CDS agreement, AIG was exposed to collateral calls. Under the contracts with its clients (those who bought the CDS), AIG agreed to put up money if the value of the securities deteriorated or AIG itself was losing its credit rating.

In late 2005, AIGFP decided to stop writing CDS on collateralized debt obligations (CDO) made up of subprime securities after the AIG Risk Management team grew concerned about the US residential real estate market.

Unfortunately for AIG, the horse was already out of the barn… In 2007, at the beginning of the summer, AIG's counterparties started asking to put up collateral (we mentioned earlier in this chapter the case of BNP Paribas which froze 1.6 € billion of funds in August 2007).

In August 2007, as part of a call with investors, Joseph Cassano said the following:

"It is hard for us, without being flippant, to even see a scenario within any kind of realm of reason that would see us losing one dollar in any of those transactions."

Throughout the rest of 2007 until September 2008, as losses mounted and the company's credit rating dropped, AIG needed to post ever more collateral until it did not have the cash to post the collateral amounts its agreements required (see the illustration 44 below). In short, AIG was in a self-fulfilling degradation of its cash position throughout 2008.

Illustration 44: Total collateral in $bn posted by AIG

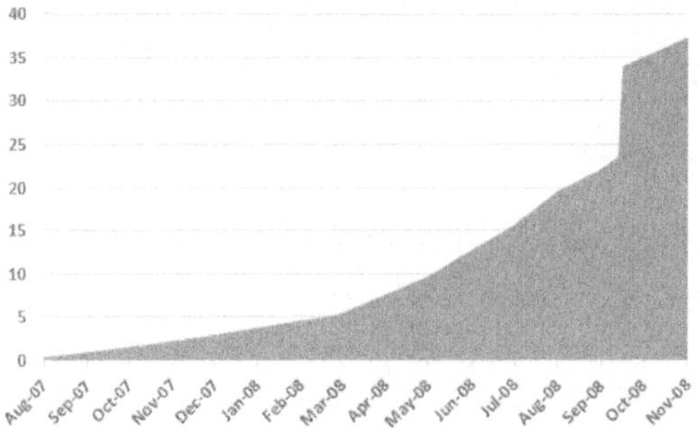

However, AIGFP was not the sole source of troubles for the firm, its problems ran deeper into AIG's regulated subsidiaries, in other words at the core of its insurance businesses.

We described the issues for AIG with their CDS activities but how about the securities lending programme. How could it go wrong? What happened?

AIG began lending securities in the early 1990s through a third-party lending agent. In 1997, AIG insourced its securities lending programme through its agent, AIG Global Asset Management Holdings Corporation.

By early 2008, AIG was a very active securities lender with an $80 billion portfolio.

Securities lending is a simple financial transaction where one institution borrows a security from another and gives a deposit of collateral, usually cash, to the lender. The collateral is in the form of cash or non-cash securities, of value equal to or higher than the loaned securities plus an agreed margin.

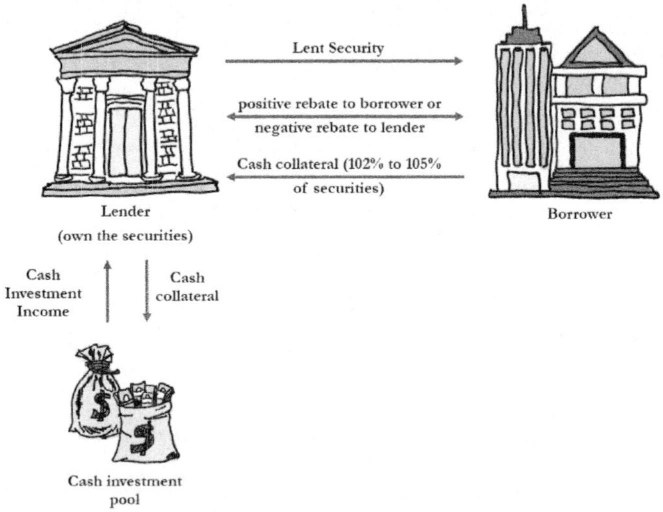

For AIG, the borrowers were providing cash collateral worth 102–105% of the value of the securities borrowed. This means that AIG was getting 2% to 5% when lending securities, which could be like earning “easy money”.

However, there is a catch. The borrower might not be able to give back the securities, thus the collaterals.

There are two primary risks with securities lending: (i) a borrower default risk and (ii) a cash collateral reinvestment risk. Borrower default risk is the risk that the counterparty fails to return the borrowed security to the lender.

With regards to the collaterals, the most significant source of risk is how the lender invests these. If it is reinvested too aggressively and results in losses, then the lender would suffer losses. This is exactly what happened with AIG.

The AIG insurance subsidiaries (life and non-life insurers) were putting their securities into a shared pool available for lending to banks, broker-dealers, and other financial institutions. AIG Global Securities Lending (GSL) was running the lending program on behalf of the AIG subsidiaries (see the illustration 45 on the next page).

There was just one "small" issue with the set-up: If AIG GSL could not return in full the borrowers' cash collateral, the participants in the programme would have to contribute with their own capital. Therefore, the AIG subsidiaries were directly exposed to the performance of the investments; they were on the hook.

Illustration 45: AIG businesses participating in the Securities-Lending Program as of the 31st of December 2007

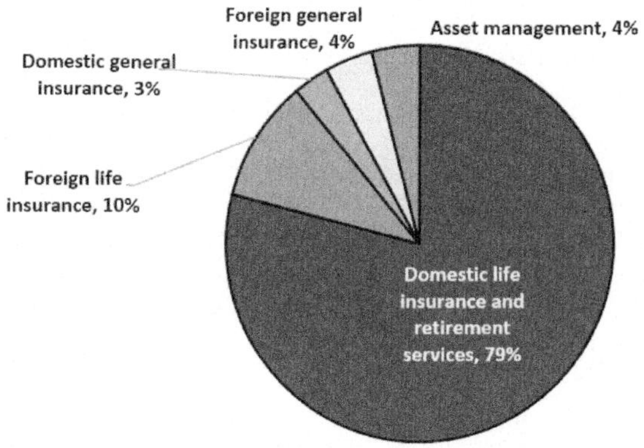

In a search for improving the yields on their investments, AIG was lending a rather high proportion of its securities (see illustration 46 below) when compared to their peers (Metlife was lending 10% of its securities).

Illustration 46: AIG Life insurance subsidiaries participating and % of their assets lent through the programme

	2007 Assets ($ Million)	% of Assets in Securities Lending
ALICO	101,632	4.5%
VALIC	63,999	15.1%
AIG Annuity	50,553	39.7%
American General Life	33,682	31.3%
SunAmerica Life	39,445	27.1%
AIG SunAmerica Life	35,072	6.1%
AIG Life	10,790	23.6%
Am General Life & Accident	9,134	33.9%
First SunAmerica	6,479	30.3%
American International	7,093	35.1%
United States Life	5,315	25.1%
Total AIG Life	**364,770**	**19.0%**

All the ingredients were in place for a terrible outcome. By summer 2007, the management of AIG was getting worried when they realised that they were at risk of experiencing a "bank run".

There was a serious risk to see the borrowers suddenly wanting their money back (their collaterals) while it was locked into "illiquid" investments.

At that stage, AIG could have decided to stop the program and sell their investments thus occurring a substantial loss. Instead, they decided to "double down" their bets with the market and increased the size of their security lending programme from $70 billion in August 2007 to $94 billion in October 2007.

At the end of 2007, 65% of AIG's securities lending collateral was invested in mortgage-backed securities, asset-backed securities, and CDOs; 19% was in corporate bonds, and 16% was in cash or other short-term investments.

So, what was bound to happen did happen, at the height of the 2008 crisis, the security lending program experienced a run, and AIG could not meet the massive repayment demands. The losses were severe, and several AIG's regulated life insurance subsidiaries were imperilled.

In June 2008, the following article was published on Bloomberg and provided some crucial details about AIG's issues with its securities lending programme.

On the 27th of June 2008 (Bloomberg) -- American International Group Inc. plans to absorb losses for a dozen insurance units after their securities-lending accounts suffered $13 billion of write-downs tied to the subprime-mortgage collapse during the past year...
... State regulatory filings show that AIG's securities-lending unit used almost two-thirds of its $78 billion in cash collateral to buy mortgage-backed securities that plunged in value starting last July as subprime defaults climbed. Most of the securities were rated AAA or AA. The market value of the collateral pool, including cash and securities, fell to $64.3 billion as of March 31.

The article showed that by March 2008, the securities lending programme lost $13.7 billion and more losses were expected for the coming summer. As AIG weakened with its net income in a nose dive, the borrowers were further pressing for their cash.

Illustration 47: AIG net income in $ billion from 2004 until the end of 2008

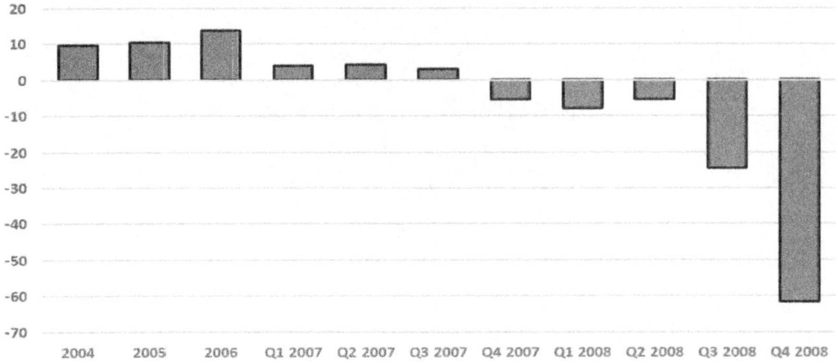

AIG was clearly in free fall without any parachute and a tough landing was expected. On the 16th of September 2008, the Federal Reserve provided an $85 billion two-year loan to AIG to prevent its bankruptcy and further stress on the global economy.

Key lessons from the AIG failure

One could wonder what would have happened if the US government let AIG go bankrupt. What would have happened to the customers' policies and assets? As mentioned earlier, lots of AIG's life insurance subsidiaries were on the hook as part of the security lending programme.

Ben Bernanke, a Former Federal Reserve Chairman, compared AIG to a hedge fund which took risks with unregulated products while using cash from people's insurance policies. It is difficult to agree with him, and we can reasonably doubt that some of the reserves set aside for the payment of claims or future claims were used in this process. The reality is that AIG's shareholders' equity and most likely some of the subsidiary capital were used to fulfil the insurance obligation (for the CDS) and to pay back the collaterals under the equity lending programme.

The capital of AIG (which we would call solvency today) was melting like the ice under the sun.

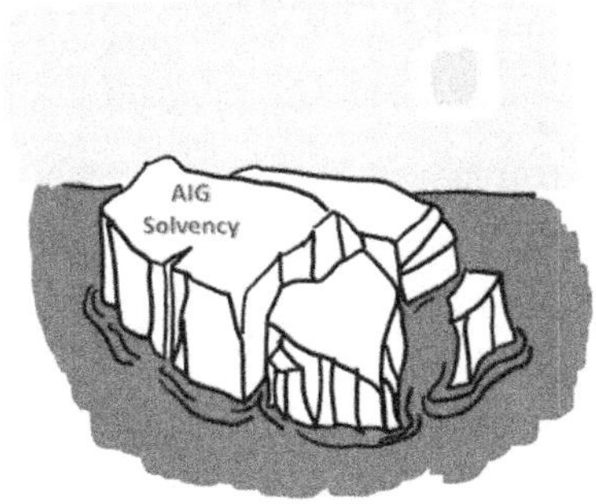

At its peak, AIG was one of the largest companies in the world, with a coveted "AAA" credit rating, over $1 trillion in assets, and 76 million customers in more than 130 countries. Unfortunately, AIG was a giant with feet of clay which could not manage its risks properly when it entered new product lines such as the Credit Default Swaps.

These **new activities were not at the core of their businesses** thus making it even more dangerous for the organization. As Warren Buffett said once "Never invest in a business, you cannot understand."

The revenues of AIGFP rose from $737 million in 1999 to $3.26 billion in 2005. The operating income at the unit also grew drastically to 17.5% of AIG's overall operating income in 2005.

The profit margins on the business were very high with 44% of revenue in 2003 and 83% in 2005. **This should have been a red flag for the management but also the financial analysts who were covering AIG**.

Unfortunately, the goose that lays the golden egg does not exist, and easy bucks often come at a dire price. AIG FP was not putting enough cash in its reserve for the risks that they were covering. There are some similarities with the case of CBL insurance mentioned earlier in this book. However, one needs to admit that regardless of the total premium being collected, AIG FP would have never been able to put aside enough reserves to cover the risks that they were covering!

It is easy to look at this after the facts and draw conclusions retrospectively. Most likely when AIG decided to enter into this line of business, the management of AIG did not have the adequate tools nor information to anticipate a collapse of the financial system and furthermore the US housing market.

It is worth mentioning that after the crisis, the new AIG management performed an amazing recovery focusing on their core business. Robert Benmosche managed to put this great organisation back on track (everyone should read his book) very rapidly.

As we have seen, uncertainty is at the core of the insurance business. As a result, insurers must manage different types of risks. The AIG case displayed what could happen when the underwriting, credit and investment management risks go wrong at the same time.

We have yet to cover the potential risk of matching assets with liabilities. This is what we will cover in the next chapter.

CHAPTER 8

THE CONSEQUENCES OF A LOW YIELD ENVIRONMENT

What are the dangers with guaranteed rates of returns?
How liabilities can sink an insurer?
What happened to the Japanese life insurers?

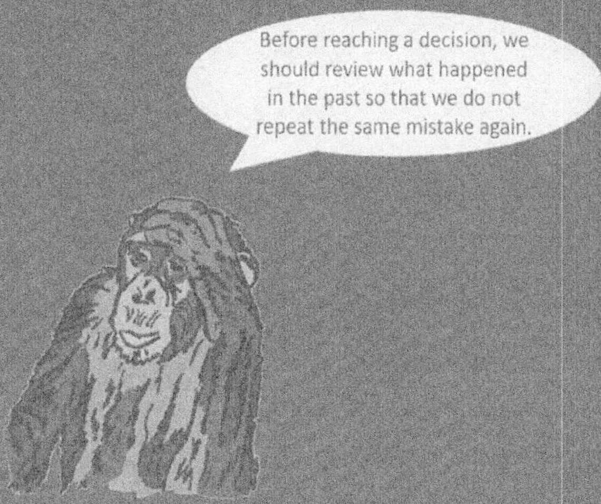

BY ERIC LEFEBVRE

Chapter Eight

Ignorance is bliss

"Speculative bubbles do not end like a short story, novel, or play ... we never know when the story is over."
– Robert Shiller

The joy of printing money? **France, 1987**

I was enjoying business and economy lectures. Our professor, Paul B was brilliant and wanted me to pursue studies in economics.

The Japanese miracle was the hot story of the time. Japanese cars and electronic items were taking the world. Paul B gave us a New York Times article about the Japanese pushing up prices of US commercial property dated 15th December 1986.

The article started with "Japanese investors have become major players in key real estate markets in the United States, snapping up hotels at Waikiki and stepping over each other to grab skyscrapers from Los Angeles to New York City."

This may ring a bell to those of us who are following what the Chinese investors were doing over the recent years throughout the western world.

Paul B did not want to focus too much on this part, he pointed us to what the Japanese life insurers were doing and why they were doing it.

As per the article, the Japanese banks and insurers had enormous sums to invest. They were managing $650 billion in 1985. Nippon Life Insurance Company, for example, had more life insurance policies in force than the three largest life insurers in the United States combined (Prudential, Metropolitan and the Equitable). These insurers had to invest their collected premiums.

Paul B used this example to cover the needs for insurers to invest their collected premiums in assets to be able to provide agreed returns to their policyholders.

Frankly speaking, it would take me two decades to fully understand the consequences of these Japanese investments which were taking place in the 1980s.

Time is flying fast especially for the insurers

In 2008, AIG was clearly at the epicentre of the CDS market crash but other insurers felt the pain in other regions. This brings us to Japan to observe the collapse of another insurer.

In October 2008, Yamato Life Insurance president Takeo Nakazono announced that his company filed for bankruptcy protection at a press conference at the Bank of Japan headquarters.

At the time, the newspapers reported that the insurer was the first credit crunch victim in Japan … this was an easy short cut to explain this failure … It is worth reviewing what happened to the life insurance industry in Japan since the 1980s to better understand what happened to Yamato.

In a desperate search for Yield – the Life insurance industry in Japan from 1980 until 2005

But first, we need to go through some history. In the 1990s, Japan went through the "lost decade" as a result of a financial crisis due to speculation which took place during a boom cycle in the 1980s. Record-low interest rates fuelled stock market and real estate speculation. Property and public company valuations were completely disconnected from the reality, Japan was experiencing an unsustainable bubble.

On the 30th of May 1989, Japan's central bank announced that it was raising its official discount rate by 0.75 percentage points to 3.25%, in the first increase in the key rate in almost a decade. Bank of Japan Governor Satoshi Sumita said the decision to raise the rate resulted from the bank's desire to stem inflation and strengthen the yen, which had fallen against the U.S. dollar.

Illustration 48: U.S. dollar / Yen exchange rate (1980 – 2003)

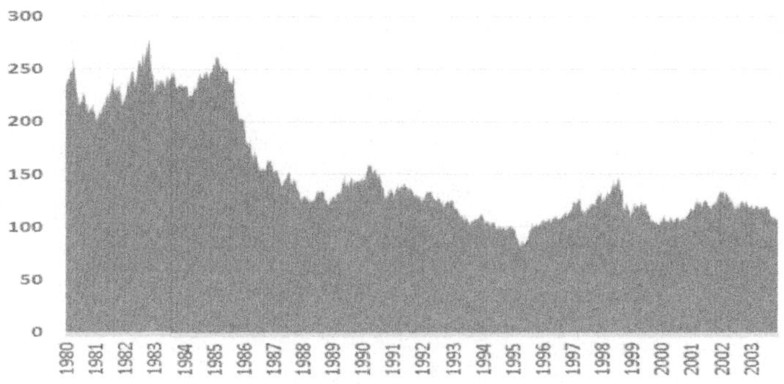

The governor also mentioned that the rate hike was a "precaution" to stem inflationary threats and stabilize prices. In less than a year, the central bank doubled the interest rates from 1989 and 1990 to end the easy credit and burst the bubble (see illustration 39 on the next page).

The move quickly led to a stock market crash and debt crisis, as borrowers failed to make payments on debts that were backed by speculative assets. In other words, people were in negative equity, something not dissimilar to what happened in the US due to the 2008 crash. From its high on 31 December 1989, the benchmark Nikkei index had dropped almost 50% by October 1990.

Illustration 49: BoJ interest rate from 1980 until 2008

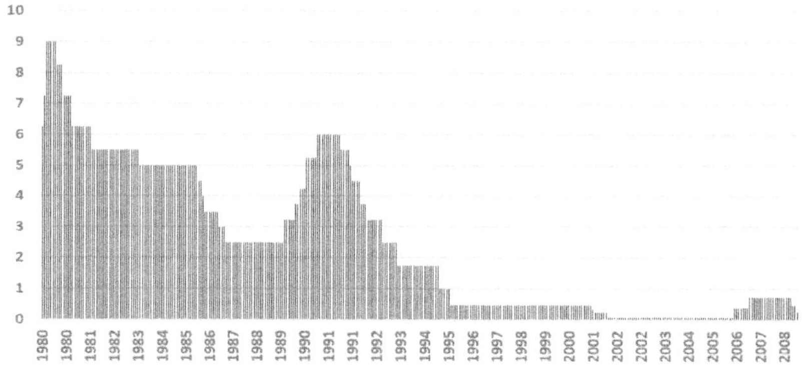

A massive deflation took place after the crash and the economy ended up in a lost decade, where the economic expansion halted for more than 10 years. During that period, the stock markets remained near record lows and the property market never fully recovered. The Nikkei index fell further over the decade and ended in 1999 at 30% of its peak value (a 70% loss). The paradox of thrift was in full play, with the Japanese saving even more than before and spending less, thus further exacerbating the deflation. The deflation encouraged further people to save more thus a deflationary spiral.

By 1999, the Japanese life insurers held 190 trillion yen in assets (roughly 160 $billion) and about 95% of Japanese households had life insurance policies. The premium income represented 40% of worldwide premiums. Everything looks good under the sun but in reality, the insurers were having a "hangover" from the booming years and several issues were plaguing their solvency.

What were the problems buried under the insurers' financial results?

Most of the problems were linked to products which were sold in the 1980s: individual life-policies that guarantee a fixed annual rate of return ranging from 5% to 6%. During this period, the insurers were trying to outbid one another in providing the highest possible rate of return.

These life insurance policies were allowing the Japanese to earn higher rates of return than the interest rates which were around 3 per cent from 1986 until 1989 (See Illustration 49 on the previous page) and throughout the 80s almost always below 6%.

To sustain these high rates of return, the Japanese life insurers had to invest in overseas bond markets and equities.

By December 1984, in a search of higher yields (see illustration 50 below), the monthly outflow of capital had soared to $8.4 billion, an annual rate of more than $100 billion. Most of the Japanese funds were invested in governmental securities (from the United States and other Western countries) but also in foreign equities.

Illustration 50: the US vs Japan interest rate in the 1980s

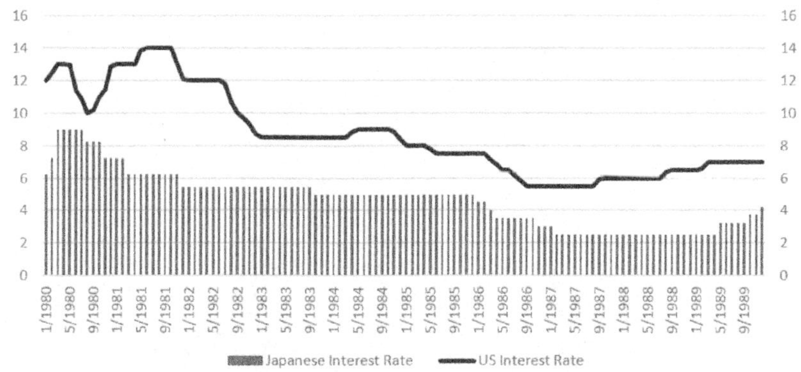

This was a smart move from the life insurers to achieve the 6% rate of return promised to their customers. This worked well at the beginning of the 1980s but ended badly for the insurers. As they did not hedge their currency risks, they got squeezed when the Yen moved against them from 1985 onwards, forcing them to swallow big losses with their capital.

We will use a simple example to illustrate how the Japanese Insurers got squeezed from the mid-eighties until the end of the eighties.

****

Example 10: Impact of the currency exchange to TokyoInsur.
By the end of 1984, TokyoInsur had collected roughly ¥500,000,000 from its customers under a 20 years endowment plan with a guaranteed annual rate of return of 6%.

In search for investment opportunities which would help them to achieve their objectives, the TokyoInsur management decides to invest 20% of this amount in 10-year US Treasury note at an auction in January 1985 with an 11.38% yield.

What is 10-year US Treasury note?
A 10-year Treasury note is a loan that a lender makes to the U.S. federal government. It has a duration of 10 years which means that for a $1,000 Treasury note with an 11.38%, the note will pay $113.8 in interest annually for 10 years before paying back at the end of the decade the $1,000.

In January 1985, the $/¥ exchange rate was ¥251.8 for one dollar. Therefore, the ¥100,000,000 brought $397,141 in 10-year Treasury note with an 11.38% interest paid annually.

$$\frac{\text{¥}100{,}000{,}000}{251.8\ \text{¥}/\$} = \$397{,}141$$

The **yearly interest** paid is **$45,195** which represents 11.38% of $397,141.

TokyoInsur were very pleased with their investment. Of course, there was a currency exchange risk but things had been stable since 1980 and they did not see any reasons for a change.

Unfortunately, 1985 was to become Annus Horribilis for the Japanese Life insurers which had invested in the US as the Japanese Yen moved against them.

Illustration 51: U.S. dollar / Yen exchange rate (1985 – 1988)

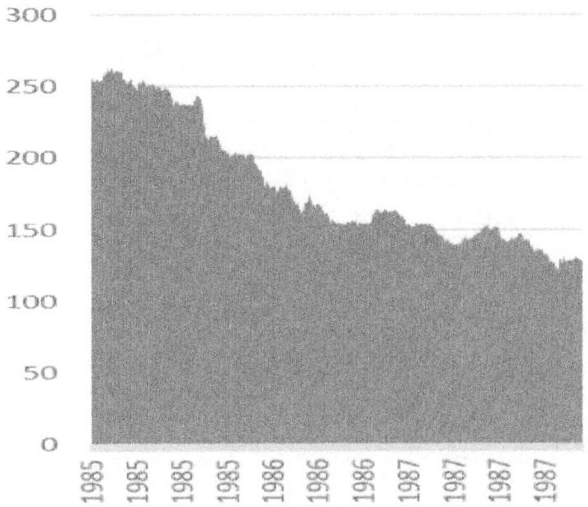

In 1985, the U.S. dollar lost 20% of its value against the Yen and by the end of 1986, the U.S: dollar lost in total 40% an important setback for TokyoInsur and any life insurer in Japan with investments in the United States.

By the end of 1985, the $/¥ exchange rate was ¥199.15 for one dollar. Therefore, the $45,145 yearly interest paid was worth ¥9,000,504 which would be a 9% gain to the initial investment. Not too bad if the value of the principal in ¥ term did not decline as well.

In one year, the $397,141 were worth ¥79,090,548, a ¥20,000,000 loss from the initial investment.

After 10 years, when including the interest earned, the initial investment of ¥100,000,000 would be ¥100,818,938. This is very far from a guaranteed 6% compound rate of return which would have provided a value of ¥179,084,770 after 10 years. Thus, a loss for the insurer of roughly ¥79,000,000 on their investment.

Principal or initial investment: $397,141	Principal or initial investment: ¥100,000,000
Total earned interest: 10 x $45,145 = $451,450	Total earned interest: Year 1 - ¥9,000,504; Year 2 - ¥7,152,045; Year 3 - ¥5,545,377; Year 4 - ¥5,586,052; Year 5 - ¥6,609,710; Year 6 - ¥6,083,193; Year 7 - ¥5,626,728; Year 8 - ¥5,667,403; Year 9 - ¥5,084,392; Year 10 - ¥4,542,961; ¥60,898,366
Value investment after 10 years: $849,087	Value investment after 10 years: ¥100,818,938

To achieve a 6% compound rate of return as per their contracts with their customers, TokyoInsur would have had to aim for a 7.75% annual rate of return, since roughly 15% of the collected premium would have been used to pay the commissions and administrative expenses.

From 1985 until 1995, the U.S. dollar lost 60% of its value against the Japanese Yen thus an important impact on the investment in U.S. Treasury note for TokyoInsur (see the illustration 52 below).

Illustration 52: Value investment in ¥ over 10 years including the interest earned.

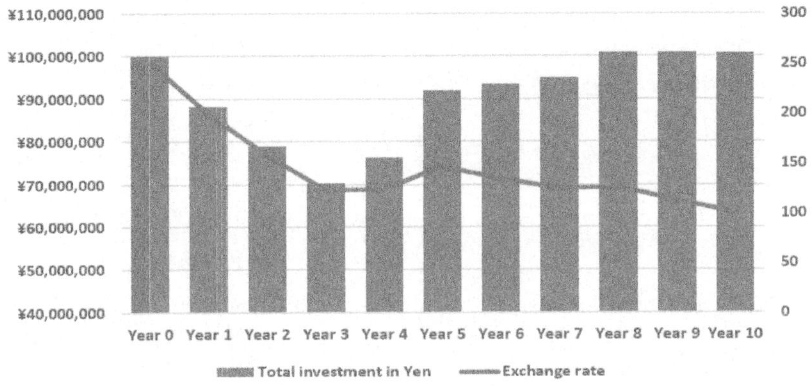

****

Our previous example illustrates the potential losses from their overseas investments for the Japanese Life insurers in the 1980s. In search of high returns, the Japanese insurers also invested in domestic and foreign equities. They got the same results for their foreign investments but some of them managed to realise good returns in Japan prior to the stock market crashed in 1990 (almost 39,000 points at its peak – see the illustration 53 below) and used these gains to absorb the losses on their overseas investments.

Illustration 53: Nikkei 225 Index from 1975 until 2005

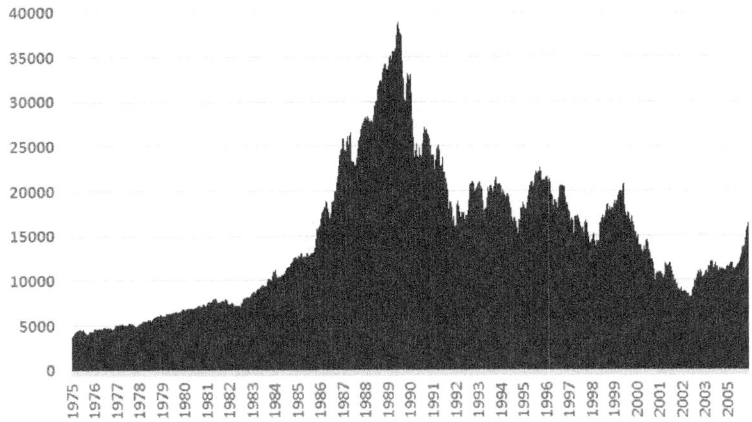

Luckily, the increase of interest rate in 1989 provided some oxygen to the Japanese insurers with a peak of 6% in 1990 still not sufficient to sustain the promised returns for the policies sold in the 1980s (see the illustration 54 on the next page) as the Japanese government bonds have a maximum duration of 10 years.

Illustration 54: BoJ interest rate 1985 - 1995

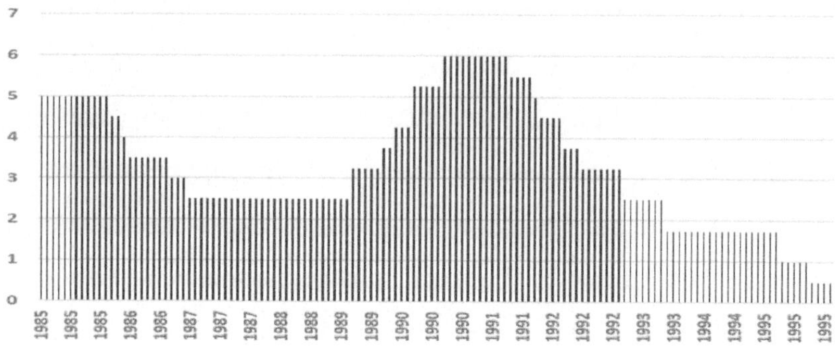

The "lost decade" did not help either the life insurers with a full-blown liquidity trap (with an interest rate at 0.5% from 1995 until 2005).

What is a liquidity trap?

A liquidity trap is a situation in which the interest rates are low and savings rates are high, rendering any monetary policy ineffective. It occurs when low/zero interest rates fail to stimulate consumer spending. This is exactly what happened in Japan during the "lost decade", any stimulus to the economy in the form of additional money was ineffective.

What happened to the guaranteed rates of return?

It took until 1993 for the insurers to start reducing their guaranteed rates of return for the new policies (see the illustration 55 below) whereas the Bank of Japan reduced its rates to 0.5% in 1995.

Illustration 55: Guaranteed rate of return vs 10-year Japanese Government Bond

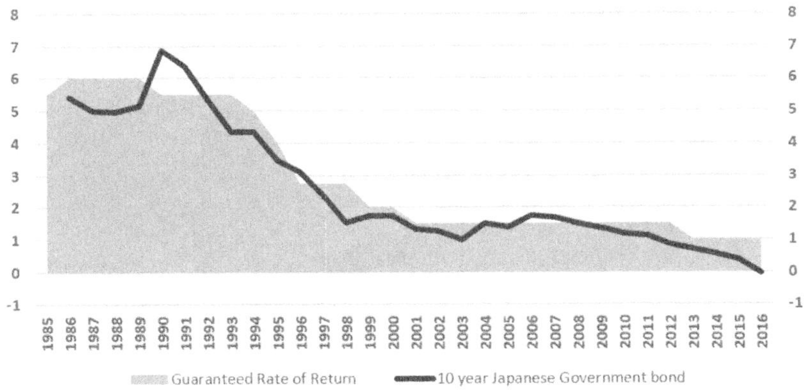

We can easily assume that with their low investment yields, some of the Japanese Life insurers had been running negative spread (Difference between the guaranteed rate of return and the interest rate) for many years (keeping in mind that a compound interest rate of 6% means a higher rate of return to be achieved to cover the distribution and administration costs).

Some experts estimated that the life insurance industry was running a "negative spread" of around 2% by the end of the "lost decade".

In one of its articles, the Economist estimated that the life-insurers' books were roughly missing a total of ¥19 trillion to ¥34 trillion ($16 billion - $28 billion) on the asset side.

As their investment yields did not match their promises, the insurers were probably not far from running a pyramid scheme where the gains on the newly issued policies could have been used to enable the high-interest rate offered for the older book of business.

Luckily for the policyholders, the insurers were very far from running a Ponzi scheme such as Bernard Madoff who followed a classic "robbing Peter to pay Paul" scenario and ended up building a net fraud of $10 to $17 billion.

The Japanese insurer did invest their customers' assets but with poor returns and somehow were matching their liabilities by digging the equivalent of a hole. And what was bound to happen did happen with the first failure of a Life Insurance Mutual at the end of the 1990s.

On the 25th of April 1997, the Japan Ministry of Finance ordered Nissan Life to suspend its business operations as its liabilities exceeded its assets by ¥300 billion ($2.4 billion). In fact, the MoF was aware that Nissan's liabilities exceeded its assets since 1993 which means that they could have stopped the insurer's operation much earlier.

The insurer was liquidated on the 1st of October 1997 when a newly created insurer: Aoba Life Insurance took over its assets and existing policies. Aoba would only manage the existing policies and would not sell new policies. The members of the Life Association of Japan created a policyholder protection fund (LIPPCJ: Life Insurance Policyholders Protection Corporation of Japan) that would cover ¥200 billion ($1.6 billion) of Nissan Life losses. The Policyholder had to absorb the remaining losses by accepting a haircut on their policies, the overall portfolio rate of return decreasing from 5.5% to 2.75%.

Nissan Life was the first life insurer to fail, in the following years, 6 additional life insurers would go down with their policyholders suffering severe cuts to their guaranteed rates of return.

Illustration 56: Bankruptcy of Japanese life insurers and excess liabilities

#	Life insurers	Date insolvency	Excess Liabilities (¥ Billion)	Excess Liabilities ($ Billion)
1	Nissan Life	Apr-97	-303	-2.40
2	Toho Life	Jun-99	-650	-5.39
3	Daihyaku Life	May-00	-318	-2.90
4	Taisho Life	Aug-00	-37	-0.34
5	Chiyoda Life	Oct-00	-595	-5.50
6	Kyoei Life	Oct-00	-690	-6.37
7	Tokyo Life	Mar-01	-73	-0.61

Kyoei Life Insurance Co ended up being the biggest corporate collapse in Japan since the Second World War with liabilities of ¥4.6 trillion ($42.6bn) and ¥3.7 trillion of assets ($34.4bn).

In April 2001, Prudential completed the takeover of the failed insurer Kyoei Life rebranded Gibraltar Life for ¥50 billion ($395 million) and provided ¥98 billion ($775 million) to Gibraltar Life in the form of a subordinated loan. As part of the restructuring, the Kyoei policyholders had to accept a 1.75% rate of return, which was much lower than the promised 4% (portfolio average).

We mentioned earlier in this chapter the case of Yamato Life which went bankrupt in 2008 because of investments in the United States had a $2.6 billion loss.

David Threadgold, a financial analyst described the case as follow: “Yamato’s been vulnerable for some time. Recent events seem to have been the straw that broke the camel’s back".

In an interview, the Finance Minister Shoichi Nakagawa mentioned that the bankruptcy was due to "Yamato's particular business strategy, and does not reflect the health of the industry as a whole … the main reason for Yamato Life's situation is its unique scheme, under which the company used proceeds from high-yielding securities to cover losses from high-cost insurance operations."

What the Finance minister forgot to mention is that the collapse of Yamato Life had its roots in the dramatic decline in the stock market from the early 1990s and the subsequent collapse of investment yields for the life insurers in Japan. Like the seven other insurers mentioned earlier, Yamato Life had most likely been suffering from a significant gap between its promised returns to its policyholders and the yield on its investments.

At the time of its collapse, Yamato Life was managing a portfolio of 180,000 life-insurance policies worth a total of 10 billion USD by the end of March 2008. As part of the restructuring plan, the average rate of guaranteed yields to individual policyholders was 1.0% and the policies transferred to Prudential's Japanese insurance unit, Gibraltar Life Insurance Co.

As part of the plan, a surrender charge of up to 20% over the following 10 years would be applied to the policyholders in the case of a contract being cancelled before its full expiration, to further reduce the returns.

Illustration 57: Guaranteed rate of return post-bankruptcy

#	Life insurers	Post bankruptcy interest rate for policyholders
1	Nissan Life	2.75%
2	Toho Life	1.50%
3	Daihyaku Life	1%
4	Taisho Life	1%
5	Chiyoda Life	1.50%
6	Kyoei Life	1.75%
7	Tokyo Life	2.60%
8	Yamato Life	1%

Are you up for a "not so free" haircut to your savings?

Key lessons from the failures of Life insurers in Japan

In Japan, market conditions were the main reason for the failure of several large insurers and a market dominated by insurance products with rather high guaranteed returns.

To fulfil their commitments of high rates of return, the Japanese life insurers had to hunt for high yields while having to deal with several events:

- An important depreciation of the USD against the Japanese Yen which led to catastrophic foreign investment in the 80s combined
- An overheated economy in the 1980s which led to a bubble bursting with falling stock and real estate prices in the early 1990s
- and the "lost decade" with stubbornly low-interest rates

The insurers ended up being in the middle of a perfect storm with negative spread problems. They used their reserves from the boom years to plug the holes in the buckets. In other words, the culprits were kicking the can down the road and still had to find a lasting solution as running a pyramid was not the right answer nor reducing their operating costs ... They eventually hit the wall and some of the insurers went out of business.

Could the insurers have resolved the problems without going bankrupt?

We need to recognise that these insurers did not have that many options since there were no long-term assets which could match the long duration of their liabilities. In addition, in the 1980s, who would have thought that (i) money would be pretty much for free from the mid-1990s onwards (with an interest rate at 0.5%) and (ii) the stock market would crash to the floor. The only solution for them was to cut the guaranteed rate of return to align the average with their investment yields, it took an orderly restructuring (via a bankruptcy process) to achieve just that (see the previous illustration 52).

As we have already covered in our previous chapters, the profitability of a life insurance policy (or product) is linked to:

1) The difference between the sold "rate of return" (assumed by the insurer for a guaranteed rate) and the "investment return" on the assets (what the insurer is getting from investing in bonds, equities, real estates, etc.)
2) The difference between (i) the death rate which was used for building the product and (ii) the actual death rate
3) The operating costs to manage the policies (assumptions versus actual)

The first factor has a prominent role in the financial health of life insurers and brought down some of the Japanese insurers

It is also worth mentioning that the Minister of Finance (MOF), which is the de facto regulator, played a prominent role in the debacle. For instance, it took 4 years for the MOF to stop Nissan Life from issuing new policies while its liabilities were exceeding its assets. To add insult to the injury, from the beginning of the 90s, it was clear to all actors that the life insurers were running a negative spread and were endangering their financial health with high guaranteed rates of return. The MOF could have stepped in and blown earlier the final whistle instead of following a "laissez-faire" approach.

Life insurers are like any financial institution, their financial results rely heavily on the interest rate and the performance of the stock market. Offering attractive savings products in a depressed market is a challenge in any country for any insurers.

Finally, the customers (policyholders) are trusting the insurers for taking good care of their savings and/or investments. After all, they are considering that the insurers are better placed than themselves to make sound investments decisions and their savings are "supposedly" safe with these institutions. The described failures remind us that Life Insurers can also go bankrupt and furthermore must be very careful when offering a guaranteed rate of return for savings products.

What the Japanese life insurers went through should provide food for thoughts to the European insurers which are currently experiencing a very similar environment than their Japanese colleagues in the 1990s.

In the wake of the 2008 financial crisis, to prop up the economy and avoid a massive recession, the western central banks went through huge monetary easing and cut drastically their interest rates. These policies pushed the bond yields to record lows in negative territories for some countries (e.g. Germany and Switzerland). As a result, many European life insurers are running the risk to have a negative spread for their old books of business.

To resolve these issues under the Solvency II regime, some German insurers chose to sell their books of businesses which were in run-off. It is to be seen if this approach is sustainable and the best option for the policyholders. As seen with the Japanese experience, it seems that the only solution is to cut the overall guaranteed rate of return unless the aggregators can sustain higher yields from their investments, this is rather "easy" in a bull market but much trickier when we will enter bear territories.

So far, to illustrate what can endanger an insurer's balance sheet we have covered (i) the case of an insurer which lost its way by trying to monetise its "AAA" rating (the proof of a solid balance sheet) and sold risky products without fully grabbing their potential impacts to its solvency and (ii) the case of liabilities literally catching the life insurers' assets and sinking some of these insurers in an embarrassing debacle for their industry.

In a world where black swan events tend to happen rather "often", we need to discuss how "relatively safe government bonds" could destroy the solvability of an insurer.

CHAPTER 9

A GROWTH STRATEGY COMBINED WITH WRONG INVESTMENTS

What happen when sovereign debts are not safe anymore?
How a wrong strategy brought an insurer to the brink of collapse?

BY ERIC LEFEBVRE

Chapter Nine

Doom and gloom

"There is only one good, knowledge,
and one evil, ignorance."
– Socrates

Where do we find the Danaides' barrel? Helsinki, July 2011

We are enjoying some days of vacation in Finland, a country close to my heart. It is always a pleasure to meet old friends and to enjoy a good hot sauna but the mood is rather low. The Euro is on everyone's lips and people are wondering if the Eurozone will survive the crisis.

Over that summer, the rumours were rife that the Deutsche Mark may be re-introduced in Germany. There was speculation that Deutsche Mark banknotes were being printed again in preparation for ditching the euro. It was said that the Bundesbank (Germany's Central bank) had been ordered to print marks as part of contingency plans to leave Europe's single currency.

I did not believe these rumours, having said this, I was not surprised to read or hear all these stories. When looking at the size of the Greek Debt to its GDP, one could only assume that that country was clearly living beyond its means. What happened in 2009, should not have come as a surprise to anyone, but until then, the European Financial Institutions were living under the assumption that Western countries or economies will never default on their debt.

Personally, I was always wondering how Greece, which was known for its olive oil and ships, could pay for its very costly 2004 Olympic games. I got an answer to my question in 2009 and thought that some of these financial institutions should have studied in detail the Greek mythology and furthermore dramas.

Their assumption that the "joy" of defaulting was limited to developing countries such as Argentina or Venezuela, appeared to be utterly wrong. The European Financial institutions which were holding a lot of the Greek government debt discovered with horror a Greek black swan.

*A **black swan** event is a metaphor that describes an event that comes as a surprise, has a major effect*

and is often inappropriately rationalized after the fact with the benefit of hindsight

On the 18th of October 2009, George Papandreou, the new Prime Minister revealed that there was a huge hole in the Greek accounts. Over the years, Greece had borrowed much more money that it could pay back through taxes and was then running a sky-high deficit (12% of its GDP). By the end of 2009, Greece's public debt amounted to roughly €300 billion, most of this debt being held by European financial institutions (See illustration 58 on the next page) with the French insurers being the most exposed (when excluding the Greek institutions).

Illustration 58: Greek debt holders by the end of 2009

#	In €Billion	Banks	Insurers	Mutual Funds, Pension, others	Total
1	Greece	55		38	93
2	**France**	**24**	**26**	**4**	**54**
3	Germany	25	8	3	36
4	Italy	7	11	8	26
5	Belgium	9	3	7	19
6	Netherlands	8	3	9	20
7	Luxembourg	8		12	20
8	Britain	11		1	12
9	Austria	5	3		8
	Total	**152**	**54**	**82**	**288**

By 2010, when it was clear that Greece will most likely default on its debt, the European banks and insurance companies started reducing their holdings of Greek government bonds pushing up the Greek bond yield (as Bond prices and yields move in opposite directions). This was the time when the golden apple of the goddess Eris was in full play.

As the days went by and more worrying information were coming from Greece, massive sell-off took place in the market with the financial institutions trying to recover as much as they can from their bonds while booking important losses. We will use an example to illustrate these losses.

****

Example 11: Greek bond prices and yields

In 2008, Insur France bought at an auction for €10,000,000 of 10-year Greek government bonds at 4.8% interest.

As we saw with our example 10, this means that every year the Greek government will pay €480,000 to Insur France which is the holder of the bonds.

In 2010, the management of Insur France gets worried about the situation in Greece and decides to reduce their exposure to the Greek government debt. Unfortunately for them, other European insurers had the same plan, thus the need to sell their bonds at a discount.

Finally, Insur France sold its bonds for €9,500,000. Even if the price is lower, the future payments of interests remain the same at €480,000. This means that the yield becomes 5.05% which is the portion of €480,000 against €9,500,000.

$$\frac{€480{,}000}{€9{,}500{,}000} = 5.05\%$$

Insur France recovered €9,500,000 and therefore made a €500,000 loss to their original investment.

Our example illustrates that when investors sell bonds, they push up the bonds' yield. The inverse is also true when the demand for bonds rises, the bonds' yield decreases.

Bond Price	Bond Yield
€2,400,000	20.00%
...	...
€9,000,000	5.33%
€9,500,000	5.05%
€10,000,000	4.80%
€10,500,000	4.57%
€11,000,000	4.36%

The yield increases when the price decreases

The yield decreases when the price increases

****

With the relation between Yield and Bond price in mind, one could only imagine the losses that the banks and insurers were incurring by 2011 when the 10-year bond yield exceeded 20%! The European Financial institutions were meeting their own "Medusa".

Adding further stress to the situation, by the end of 2011, under a push from the Eurozone leaders, the European banks and insurers agreed with a 50% loss on their Greek government bonds.

Early 2012, when these institutions revealed their results for 2011, we could get a better view of their losses with the French banks and insurers having the lead. In compliance with European agreements, most of the institutions wrote down the Greek bonds in their portfolio by 70% (see the illustration 59 below for the banks and insurers).

Illustration 59: Losses on Greek bonds by end of 2011 for major European banks and insurers

#	Entities	Losses on Greek bonds (€ billion)	Countries	Bank / Insurer
1	BNP Paribas	3.5	France	Bank
2	**Groupama**	**2.9**	**France**	**Insurer**
3	Dexia	2.5	France / Belgium	Bank
4	Credit Agricole	2.4	France	Bank
5	Generali	2.3	Italy	Insurer
6	Commerzbank	2	Germany	Bank
7	Royal Bank of Scotland	1.4	UK	Bank
8	CNP Assurances	1.4	France	Insurer
9	Societe Generale	0.66	France	Bank
10	Allianz	0.65	Germany	Insurer
11	Deutsche Bank	0.4	Germany	Bank
12	Axa	0.39	France	Insurer

Thanks to their size, some of these institutions managed the "write-off" without major consequences (e.g. BNP Paribas, Credit Agricole, CNP Assurances), whereas weaker institutions either disappeared like Dexia which received a bailout by the end of 2011 or the French Insurer Groupama which became almost insolvent.

Throughout 2011, the financial results from Groupama were alarming with several profit warnings and furthermore a solvency ratio which was getting weaker and weaker. Their 2011 financial close got delayed ensuring that their solvency ratio remained above 100% with the help of the French state and the regulator, which played the role of Chrono. They announced a €1.8 billion loss for the Financial Year 2011 because of several impairments putting the emphasis on the Greek debt crisis.

But as always when digging into the financial results of a firm, we can find very interesting facts which lead to a different picture.

The frog that wished to be as big as the Ox

At the end of the 1990s, Groupama bought Gan Assurances from the French State. This transaction provided the mutual insurer with a very good platform for its future development.

Following this, under the management of his new CEO, Jean Azema, Groupama had the ambition to be in the top 10 of the European insurance industry by the following decade. It wanted to play in the same league than the other big French financial institutions (i) the bank Credit Agricole and furthermore (ii) the largest insurer Axa.

To achieve this, in 2001, they entered into a partnership with a French bank: La Société Générale to create a bank online: Groupama Banque. Those were the years where all the advisers were talking about the necessary convergence between banking and insurance. They were advising insurers to create bank online from scratch with rather mixed results. As part of their collaboration with Société Générale, Groupama bought some shares in the bank and ended up being the main shareholder with 4.9% of their shares (the price per share was 56€).

Through the 2000s, in addition to Société Générale, Groupama rushed headlong with other important equity investments in several flagships such as the French Veolia with 5.7% (paid 28 euros), 6.7% in Eiffage but also 4.9% in the Italian Mediobanca. Their aggressive investments in Equities could be seen in their asset portfolio breakdown. By the end of 2011, the equities were representing 15% of their portfolio whereas the standard for the French industry was around 5% to 7%. In other words, Groupama was pursuing a very risky capital allocation.

But important investments with some big European flagships was not enough, from 2005 onwards, Jean Azema had "grand plan" for the dusty insurer. He wanted to accomplish what their arch-rival

Credit Agricole managed to do in 2001: a partial IPO of the group. In 2006, the Groupama SA general assemblée agreed with this strategy and gave the green light to the CEO for introducing 20 to 25% of their capital to external investors via an IPO. The proceeds would be used to finance the international expansion of Groupama.

It did not take long for Groupama to start a buying spree with its first acquisitions in the UK and Turkey. Over the following years, Groupama bought small and medium-sized insurers (and/or created Greenfield insurance operations in Asia) in Southern and Eastern Europe spending more than €3billions in a very short time. This includes a whopping single transaction of €1.2 billion in Italy which took place in 2007.

Illustration 60: Groupama transactions taking place in 3 years for a total exceeding €3 billion.

Year	Purchase	Countries	€m	Total €m
2006	Basak Sigorta	Turkey	222	442
	Carole Nash	UK	120	
	Azur Multiramos and Azur Vida	Spain	100	
2007	Phoenix Metrolife	Greece	96	1,684
	BT Asigurari	Romania	100	
	Bollington Group	UK	100	
	Lark Group	UK	50	
	Nuova Tirrena	**Italy**	**1,250**	
	17.35% of CEGID	France	88	
2008	Asiban	Romania	350	1,219
	35% voting rights in Société Tunisienne d'Assurances et de Réassurances (Star)	Tunisia	72	
	Güven Sigorta and Güven Hayat	Turkey	180	
	OTP Garancia Biztosító	Bulgaria Hungaria Slovakia	617	

We can see in their annual reports from 2004 until 2008, a sharp increase to the Goodwill which shows that these acquisitions were paid at a very high premium. For instance, they bought Nuova Tirrena from Generali in 2007 for €1.25 billion which was a rather high price for a business which delivered a net income of €32 million in 2006. Groupama valued the business at 1.54 time the total income of €814 million. In total for €3.3 billion of acquisition, the goodwill increased by €2.3billion (see the illustration 61 below). These transactions could hamper the future results of the firm when they must impair their goodwill.

Illustration 61: Groupama goodwill from 2003 until 2012

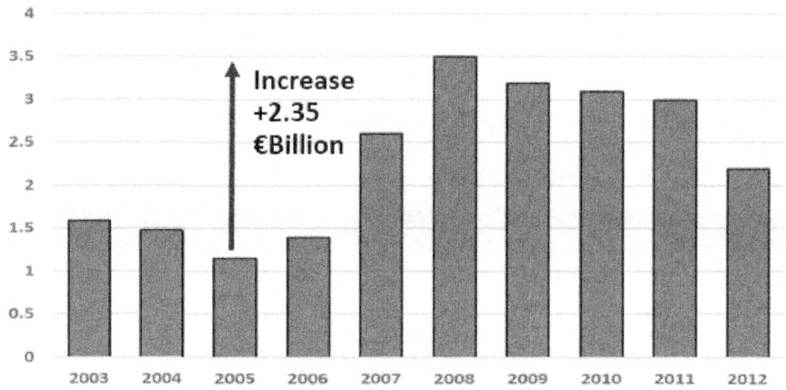

At the beginning of 2011, Groupama kept pursuing its growth strategy even if the potential storm clouds were not a long way off.

It announced that it was interested in buying a stake of up to 20% in Italian insurer Fondiaria-SAI, Italy's second-largest insurer. They mentioned that the acquisition was dependent on market conditions and regulatory approval. Finally, Groupama did not go through with this acquisition.

This missed transaction would be the twilight of Groupama's growth ambitions. As described earlier, all the ingredients were in place for the perfect storm: (i) investments in distressed Eurozone government bonds (Greece, Spain, Italy, etc.), (ii) bigger than average investments in equities, and (iii) very pricey international acquisitions in preparation for a future IPO.

In May 2011, taking into consideration the insurer's material exposure to Greek government bonds, "Standard & Poor's (S&P) downgraded Groupama's financial strength rating from A- to BBB+. This may not sound very important but a rating below A- is considered a handicap to an international insurer. Some reinsurance contracts have "downgrade clauses" and a below A- grade could provide the option for a reinsured to end a contract.

The agency was anticipating that the Greek sovereign debt crisis would weaken Groupama's capital adequacy in other words, its solvency ratio. The rating agency held out little prospect of Groupama recovering its A- rating in the near term. "We believe it is unlikely that Groupama's capital adequacy under our model will recover to the levels supportive of strong financial strength ratings in the next two years".

Climbs are spectacular
Downfalls disgraceful

Groupama was the first big European insurer to suffer capital adequacy problems because of the sovereign debt crisis. Over the following months, Groupama's credit rating kept being downgraded and in a year time, it reached the "junk bonds" territory (see illustration 62 below).

Illustration 62: Groupama long-term debt rating downgraded to junk bond in two years (Standard&Poor's)

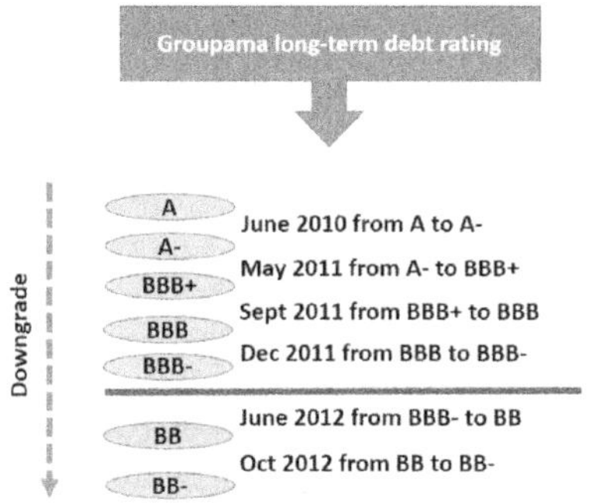

Bond rating	Grade	Capacity to pay back
AAA	Investment bonds	Extremely Strong
AA+, AA, AA-		Very Strong
A+		Strong
A		Strong
A-		Strong
BBB+		Adequate
BBB		Adequate
BBB-		Adequate
BB+	Speculative or Junk Bonds	Faces major future uncertainties
BB		Faces major future uncertainties
BB-		Faces major future uncertainties
B		Faces major uncertainties
CCC		Faces major uncertainties

As we saw earlier in this chapter the Greek debt was only part of the problem for Groupama. For the Financial Year 2011, its portfolio of shares was frittering and whittling away, stressing further their solvency ratio (€900m of value gone in 2011).

In the second half of 2011, Groupama was desperately looking for cash to maintain its solvency ratio above 100%. Its total shareholders' equity was melting fast from €7 billion by the end of 2010 to 5.3 billion at the end of 2011, more than €2 billion gone up in smoke.

With the help of the French state, Groupama managed to keep its solvency ratio above 100% by the end of 2011 (it was most likely below 100% during the last quarter of 2011). La Caisse des depots (owned by the French state) saved Groupama by injecting €300 million against preferred shares from Gan Eurocourtage and took over some of Groupama's shares in Silic. These two financial transactions helped Groupama to maintain its solvency ratio just above 100% (see illustration 63 on the next page).

Illustration 63: Groupama solvency ratio and shareholders' equity (in €billion)

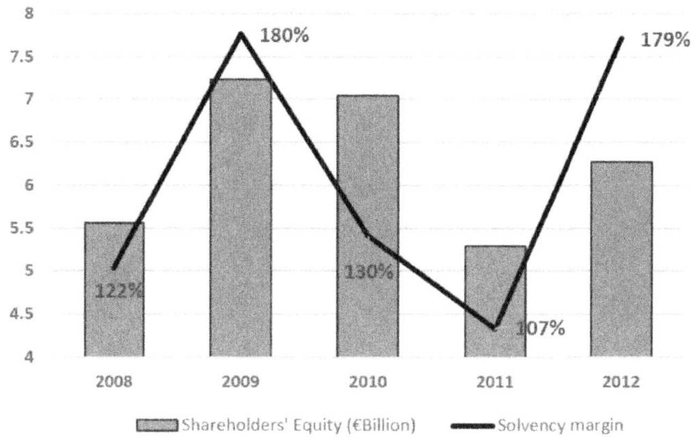

Clearly, the priority for Groupama in 2011 was to keep its solvency ratio above 100% while the value of its assets was shrinking thus selling the jewellery. Through all the sales of its assets and the disposals of shares, Groupama was hoping to recover €1.8 billion in cash (see the illustration 64 below).

Illustration 64: Groupama disposal of assets

Year	Assets sold	Buyer	Country	Transactions (€Million)	Total (€ Million)
2012	Gan Eurocourtage	Allianz	France	100	
2012	Groupama Insurance	Aegas	UK	140	
2012	Polish Proama	Generali	Poland	60*	
2012	Groupama Seguros	Grupo Catalana Occidente	Spain	400	1,200
2012	Prime Building on the Champs Elysee	Qatar	France	500	
2013	Groupama Private Equity	ACG Private Equity	France	100*	
2013	Societe Generale shares		France	520	1,020
2013	SILIC shares	Caisse des depots	France	400*	

*Estimates

The fire sale of assets did not avoid Groupama's credit rating to fall into junk territories in June 2012 (see previous illustration 62).

In October 2012, to add insult to injury, Groupama decided to skip a coupon on a 1 €billion of subordinated bonds (a payment of 60 €million for the interests). Groupama argued that the move did not constitute an event of default as they wanted to get their lenders to contribute to their restructuring efforts. The rating agencies rightly did not agree with Groupama's position and cut further the rating of their debts.

Be happy like Sisyphus

It would take two years for Groupama to get back into positive territories for its net income with a staggering 1.8 €Billion loss in 2011 and a 600 €million loss in 2012 (see Illustration 65 on the next page). Not to mention the 2.2 €billion of assets sold in 2011 and 2012, we can conclude that Groupama paid a heavy price for its ambition to become a major financial services player in Europe.

Illustration 65: Groupama net income in €Million

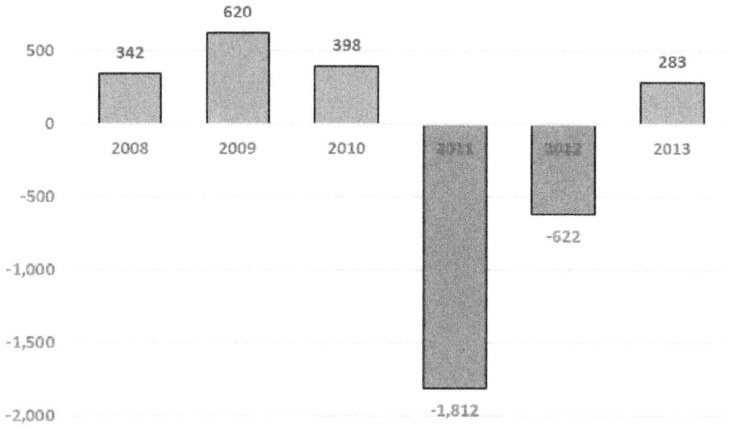

It is worth mentioning that in December 2012, Groupama decided that they would not allow Standard & Poor's to rate their debt anymore. They decided to keep just one agency Fitch rating, arguing that Standard & Poor's did not understand the nature of their business and their mutual structure.

Key lessons from the failure of Groupama in France

From the beginning of the Eurozone, it was obvious that the Greek sovereign debt was not as safe as the German bunds especially when knowing that Greece has been in default for 50% of its time as an independent country. Greece was known to be a country where tax evasion is described as "a national sport" with up to €30 billion per year going uncollected. Therefore, we can question why some of the European financial institutions decided to buy a lot of the Greek sovereign debt, the only explanation being a higher yield compared to the German bunds or even the French bonds (50 basis points higher on average from 2001 until 2008).

Groupama was not the only financial institution to get caught with too much of the Greek debts on its book but its share of distressed debt relative to its total assets was much higher than for any other French institution thus their own credit rating being very exposed to the downgrade of the sovereign debts.

As we all know, it never rains but it pours. Therefore, it was not a total surprise to see the succession of bad news for Groupama in 2011. When looking at their annual reports from the previous years, we could have seen that in a quest for size, they were on a buying spree, paying far too much for a collection of assets in different countries. The 3 €billion used for the acquisition were direly missing in 2011 when a hole appeared in their capital.

In fact, with this amount, Groupama would have weathered very well the Greek debt crisis and kept a solvency ratio well above 150%. Instead, they had to go through a fire sale to save their solvency and posted two years of losses. During the same period, Allianz, Axa or Zurich managed to keep a high solvency ratio without many efforts.

Clearly, Groupama had bitten off more than it could chew and we can see that the management decisions from the early 2000s had dire consequences for the firm a few years later. Luckily for the Groupama's clients, the French state decided that the insurer was "too big to fail" thus a rescue by the end of 2011 via La Caisse des Depots. For Groupama, the Greek sovereign debt crisis was the tree that hid the forest of problems.

This case shows that the solvency ratio of insurers is very fragile and in time of stress, their assets could deplete rapidly. The wrong allocation of assets can wipe out their capital and render them insolvent very quickly.

We saw in this chapter how the wrong allocation of assets can bring an insurer to its knees. The quest of yield to fulfil promises made to customers could have dramatic consequences. But how do we know if an insurer is following the right strategy? This is what we will see in our next chapter, we will provide the tools to be used to assess the performance of an insurer against its peers.

CHAPTER 10

TOOLS TO ASSESS THE FINANCIAL PERFORMANCE OF AN INSURER

How to read an insurer's balance sheet?
What are the Key Performance Indicators for insurance companies?
What is the performance of Berkshire Hathaway?

BY ERIC LEFEBVRE

Chapter Ten

All is number

"Details create the big picture"
– Sanford I. Weill

Is it really that good? – Zurich, Spring 2011

I had been working with Zurich Financial Services for several months and our CEO was announcing the 2010 financial results with a business operating profit of almost 5 $billion. My colleagues were all very pleased with these results, yes there was a decrease of 10% compared to the previous year but the dividend remained the same at 17CHF per share. Finally, the Return on Equity was still rather high at 12.9%. My colleagues knew that their bonus would be good and felt that Zurich was following the right strategy with profitable growth, not to mention that some of them had been with Zurich for many years thus had an interesting number of shares which would give them several thousands of francs when the dividends would be paid out.

In his letter, Martin Senn declared:
"The headline figures for 2010 were affected by an above-average frequency of large loss events and other items, and mask the underlying profitability of our businesses.
Our operating businesses remain sound with a continued focus on driving growth and value in Global Life and Farmers, and in General Insurance, achieving selected growth in those areas where we can do so profitably."

When I read the letter, and listened to our CEO, I thought that it was omitting several key performance indicators.

I must admit that I already gain an interesting reputation with some of my colleagues, when I pointed out that "an above-average frequency of large loss events" was a bad excuse and "selected growth" meant nothing. Indeed, a 5 $billion business operating profit was a big amount but this needed to be measured against the total income which was roughly 68 $billion, thus an operating margin of 7%.

This was a good margin when compared to other insurers, Axa for that year had a 3.5% margin and Allianz posted almost an 8% margin.

With all the numbers that are made available in an annual report, how do we know if the performance of an insurer is good? Is a 5 $Billions operating profit an excellent result? This chapter will be all about lifting the veil on the complexity of insurers.

How to demystify the insurers' activities?

As we have seen in previous chapters, the insurers are somehow acting like wizards or alchemists with their capabilities to create money out of their machinery.

If used correctly, the compound interest rate is making their fortune. As stated earlier, the insurance float is a borrowing facility to fund the insurers' investments.

As a reminder, the insurance float is the difference between the collected premiums and the claims which will be paid at some point. If the claims are not paid out, the collected premium can be invested in certain asset classes. When an insurer can run an underwriting profit, it effectively gets paid to invest "cash" and earn an investment income. When the insurer is running an underwriting loss, the loss is the interest paid by the insurer for the "collected cash" that he can invest.

We should keep in mind these when assessing the performance of non-life insurers. To summarise, we are assessing the skills of their management team to effectively run the "factory" which produces cash.

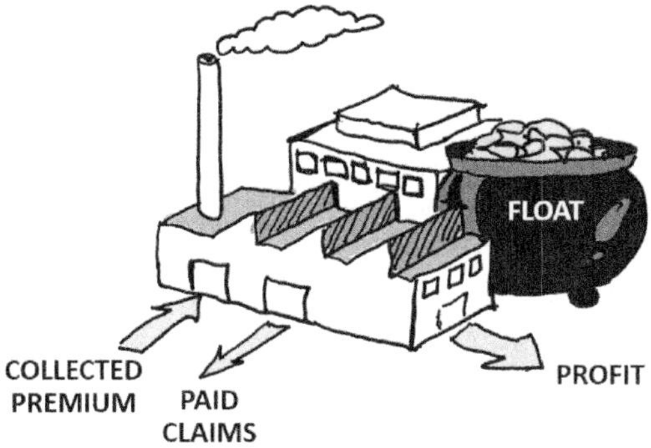

The cash collected from different sources (Policyholders, lenders and shareholders) is used to cover the expenses (claims, claims expenses, vendors' expenses) and finance the insurer's operations (employees' salaries, Information technology, buildings, maintenance, etc.) but also the interest payment for the debt.
Hopefully, in the end, all these produce a profit. The profit could be used to pay the shareholders' dividend, to increase the shareholders' equity or to invest in the future of the firm.

But where do we find in an annual report the information which will help us to assess the performance of an insurer?

We will use an example to illustrate what could be gathered 1) from an insurer's financial statement and 2) its balance sheet.

****

Example 12: Progressive financial results for the years 2015, 2016 and 2017 – in $Millions

For the years ended December 31, 2017

REVENUES	2,017	2,016	2,015
Net premiums earned	25,730	22,474	19,899
Investment income	563	479	455
Net realized gains (losses) on securities:			
Net impairment losses recognized in earnings	*-65*	*-87*	*-24*
Net realized gains (losses) on securities	*114*	*138*	*137*
Total net realized gains (losses) on securities	50	51	113
Fees and other revenues	371	333	302
Service revenues	127	103	86
Other gains (losses)	-1	2	-1
Total revenues	**26,839**	**23,441**	**20,854**
EXPENSES	**2,017**	**2,016**	**2,015**
Losses and loss adjustment expenses	18,808	16,880	14,342
Policy acquisition costs	2,125	1,864	1,652
Other underwriting expenses	3,481	2,972	2,712
Investment expenses	24	22	23
Service expenses	110	92	78
Interest expense	153	141	136
Total expenses	**24,700**	**21,971**	**18,942**
NET INCOME			
Income before income taxes	2,139	1,471	1,912
Provision for income taxes	541	414	611
Net income	**1,598**	**1,057**	**1,301**

This is a simplified version of an insurers' income statement but it already provides us with some information: their total income, the share of investment income, their loss and combined ratio, the operating margin but also insurance margin. Finally, we can see that their earnings are reducing faster than their collected premium and/or total income.

What is their Operating Margin?

The Operating margin is a measure of profitability. It indicates how much of each dollar of revenues is left over after both costs of goods sold and operating expenses are considered.

The formula to compute the operating margin is as follow:

$$Operating\ Margin = \frac{Operating\ Earnings}{Revenue}$$

For 2017, the operating margin was:

$$\frac{2{,}139}{26{,}839} = 8\%$$

What is Progressive's Insurance Margin?

As mentioned earlier, insurers hold a "float" and the insurance margin is derived from this.

The formula to compute the insurance margin is as follow:

$$Insurance\ Margin = \frac{Insurance\ Profit}{Net\ Earned\ Premium\ (NEP)}$$

For 2017, the insurance margin was:

$$\frac{2{,}139}{25{,}730} = 8.3\%$$

What is Progressive's underwriting profit?

The underwriting profit represents the earned premium after the claims benefits and administrative expenses have been paid. It does not include any investment income earned from the float, which means that we are also excluding the expenses associated with these investments.

The formula to compute the underwriting profit is as follow:

$$Underwriting\ Profit = Earned\ Premium - (Claims\ Benefits + Administative\ Expenses)$$

An underwriting loss implies that the insurer's results will rely mostly on the performance of its investments.

An underwriting profit means that the clients are providing for free the investment float.

For 2017, Progressive ran an underwriting gain, thus managing for free an investment float:

$$25{,}730 - (18{,}808 + 2{,}125 + 3{,}481) = 1{,}316$$

What is Progressive's Claims Ratio?

The claims ratio (also called loss ratio) is the ratio of total losses incurred in claims plus adjustment expenses divided by the total premiums earned.

$$Claims\ ratio = \frac{Total\ losses + adjustment\ expenses}{Total\ earned\ premium}$$

The lower the ratio, the better it is for the overall profitability.

In 2017, InsuR ran a good loss ratio:

$$\frac{18{,}808}{25{,}730} = 73.1\%$$

What is their expense ratio?

The expense ratio applies for the insurance operation and does not represent the investment activities of an insurer. We calculate this ratio by dividing the expenses for acquiring (e.g. brokers' commissions), underwriting and managing the insurance policies by the net earned premiums.

$$Expense\ Ratio = \frac{Total\ Underwriting\ and\ Operating\ Expenses}{Net\ Earned\ Premium\ (NEP)}$$

In 2017, Progressive ran the following expense ratio:

$$\frac{(2{,}125 + 3{,}481)}{25{,}730} = 21.8\%$$

The expense ratio represents an insurer's efficiency before taking into consideration the claims on the written policies and investment gains or losses.

What is the combined ratio?

A combined ratio represents the profitability of an insurer when the results of its investments are excluded.

It is the ratio of total costs divided by total revenue. In other words, it is the combination of the expense ratio and the loss ratio.

$$Combined\ ratio = Loss\ ratio + Expense\ ratio$$

In 2017, Progressive ran the following combined ratio:

$$73.1\% + 21.8\% = 94.9\%$$

A combined ratio above 100% means that an insurance company had more losses plus expenses than earned premiums and lost money on its insurance operations. A combined ratio below 100% means that the insurer is earning money on its insurance operations.

So, the results for Progressive look good, but like any insurers, we should always go through the annual report to find the necessary information for assessing the true performance of the business, as always, the devil is in the details…

When exploring their annual report, we can see that their Property line of business had a combined ratio of 105% in 2017, in other words, these operations lost cash. This was the result of the Hurricane Irma and Harvey but also severe thunderstorms in the US. These events contributed to an aggregated loss of 32.4% to the total property premium.

For Progressive, we have the following performance indicators:

	31/12/2017	31/12/2016	31/12/2015
Operating Margin	8.0%	6.3%	9.2%
Insurance Margin	8.3%	6.5%	9.6%
Underwritting gain or loss	1,316	759	1,193
Expense Ratio	21.8%	21.5%	21.9%
Loss Ratio	73.1%	75.1%	72.1%
Combined ratio	94.9%	96.6%	94.0%

We can easily see that Progressive's performance for its non-life insurance business is very good and rather consistent.

****

When assessing the financial performance of an insurer, we should not take the indicators in isolation. It is important to benchmark any insurer against its peers. In addition, in our example, we can only come up with few conclusions, we must gather much more information from the annual reports e.g. geographies, product mix, and performance per business line: general insurance (Individuals, commercial, corporate), life insurance, asset management, etc.

Based on the previous case studies on insurers' failures, we also know that for insurers, it takes many years to see the impacts of major strategic decisions to the results of an insurer. Therefore, the review of the financial results should be done over several years (five to ten years) to identify the patterns and assess the performance of the management team which evolves over time.
In addition, the length of the review will also help us to understand whether the insurers are managing well their business cycles.

As we all know the financial statements are only providing a part of the story, we also need to check the insurers' balance sheet. All the available information might sound Greek, thus the need to come back to the basics to get to what we need when assessing the performance of an insurer and its management team!

We shall remind that we are after the insurers' "holy grail", the float and this is exactly what we are trying to find out from the balance sheet.

But what to do with the balance sheet to come up with the float? As described in our previous chapters, the "float" is the cash collected from the customers, which has not been paid out for claims and expenses. It represents the claims reserves and the premium reserves.

The following formula could be used to estimate the float of an insurer.

+ Loss reserves / unpaid losses
+ liabilities vis-à-vis policyholders
+ unearned premium reserves (UPR)
– premium receivables
– reinsurance-related receivables
– deferred policy acquisition costs

= Float

But it could get very difficult to find the necessary information in the annual report of an insurer.

The balance sheet of an insurer often shows lots of information such as "cash & cash equivalents", "goodwill", "tangible and intangible assets", receivables, shareholders' equity but what shall we do with these items?

As we did with the income statement, we will use an example to illustrate how to calculate the float. We will follow an effective approach which was described in the "motley fool" some years ago.

****

Example 13: Progressive balance sheet for the years 2017 and 2016

ASSETS (in $Million)	2017	2016
Investments — Available-for-sale, at fair value:		
Fixed maturities	20,202	16,244
Equity securities:		
Nonredeemable preferred stocks	804	854
Common equities	3,400	2,812
Short-term investments	2,869	3,573
Total investments	**27,275**	**23,483**
Cash and cash equivalents	265	212
Restricted cash	10	15
Total cash, cash equivalents, and restricted cash	**275**	**226**
Accrued investment income	120	104
Premiums receivable	5,423	4,509
Reinsurance recoverables and loss adjustment expenses	2,273	1,885
Prepaid reinsurance premiums	203	171
Deferred acquisition costs	781	651
Property and equipment	1,120	1,177
Goodwill	453	449
Intangible assets	367	433
Other assets	413	340
Total assets	**38,701**	**33,428**
LIABILITIES (in $Million)		
Unearned premiums	8,904	7,468
Loss and loss adjustment expense reserves	13,087	11,368
Net deferred income taxes	135	111
Dividends payable	655	395
Accounts payable, accrued expenses, and other liabilities	2,826	2,496
Debt	3,306	3,148
Total liabilities	**28,913**	**24,987**
REDEEMABLE NONCONTROLLING INTEREST	504	484
SHAREHOLDERS' EQUITY	9,285	7,957
Total liabilities, redeemable NCI, and shareholders' equity	**38,701**	**33,428**

Simplification is the leitmotif for what we need to do – we must simplify the balance sheet and find what we are looking for: the money that the insurer has collected from its clients but has not yet used to pay claims.

From the assets side, we need to group all investments together especially those which provide an investment return. To do so, we must go through the annual report to check what every listed item cover.

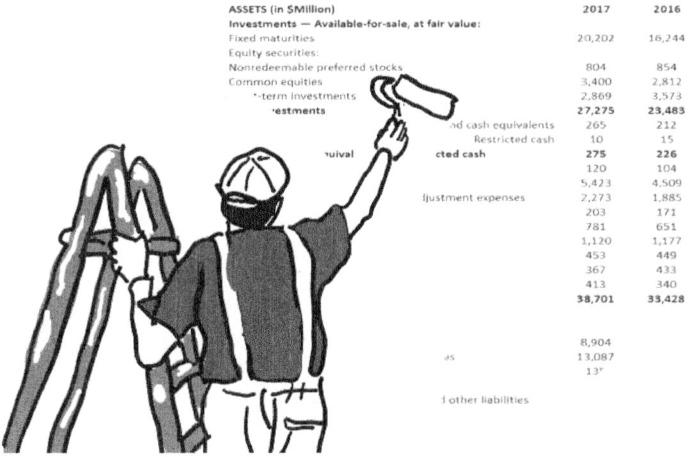

The intangible assets are covering investments in software but could also be trademarks, thus could not be considered in this case as producing an investment income. We will group them in “assets which do not produce an investment income”.

The property and equipment are tangible assets but do not help us either as they represent the fair value of the properties used by the firm to run its activities but also the furniture and/or other materials used for the insurance operations. We will not consider these items as producing an investment income and will add them with the intangible assets. To this category, we will also add the "goodwill" which do not produce any income either but could negatively impact the assets of an insurer.

Total assets without investment income for 2017: 1,939 $Millions

We will keep the "investments" category "as is". This groups the equity instruments, fixed income instruments, preferred stocks which are used to produce an investment income. We will add to this the cash and the "accrued investment income".

Total investment for 2017: 27,670 $Millions

The receivables provide the amounts which are owed to the insurer either by its clients (the policyholders) but also the reinsurers or because of financial derivatives.

For the float, on the "asset side" of the balance sheet, what we are really after is the policyholder's cash that the insurer has not yet in its bank account (coming either from the direct clients but also through the reinsurance operations)!

We can see the "premiums receivable" but also the "receivables arising out of reinsurance operations". We can also see "Prepaid reinsurance premiums" which refer to money already paid to reinsurers for future reinsurance policies. We will add these items together.

In 2017, the total amount of cash linked to "sold policies" which was to be recovered was therefore 5,423 $Millions + 2,273 $Million + 203 $Million = 7,899 $Million.

We are not done yet with the asset side of the balance sheet. There is another item which impacts the "float": the commissions paid to the distributors while the clients have not yet paid their premium and/or the premium has not been fully earned. We can find this under the item "Deferred acquisition costs".

The "deferred acquisition costs" refer to the practice of deferring the cost of acquiring a new customer over the duration of the insurance contract.

In 2017, the deferred acquisition costs were 781 $Millions.

In 2017, the total amount of cash from the clients which was not in the insurer's "coffer" will be: 8,899 $Millions + 781 $Millions = 8,680 $Millions.

In 2017, the simplified view of the assets is therefore as follow:

1) Total assets without investment income: 1,939 $Millions
2) Total investments producing an income: 27,670 $Millions
3) Total insureds' cash not with the insurer: 8,680 $Millions
4) Other assets: 413 $Millions

Total assets: 38,701 $Millions

With regards to the float, we need to identify on the "liabilities" side of the balance sheet, the cash that the insurer has received from the policyholders but not yet used for its operations and/or claims payments. This is the insureds' money sitting on the insurer's bank account.

As mentioned with the review of the assets, we must go through the annual report to find the necessary information, as often, the devil is in the details…

For the float, we are looking at the premium which has not been earned yet. As mentioned in one of our previous chapters, the "unearned premium" is the premium which relates to the time remaining on an insurance policy. If a policyholder cancels her policy, the insurer would pay her back this portion of the premium minus the administration costs. As a result, we are seeing the "unearned premium" as a liability for the insurer.

"Unearned premium" does not mean that the cash is not in the insurer's coffers. This cash is usually invested in short-term securities, thus bringing an investment income for progressive at almost no costs. As per its balance sheet, in 2017, Progressive had 8,904 $Millions of unearned premiums.

Another liability which can be found in the insurer's balance sheet can generate an investment income: The reserve for claims! This represents cash which is earmarked for incurred claims that have not been settled but also the IBNR (Incurred but not reported). The claims reserve is usually invested in very liquid assets such as short term, guaranteed, low-interest vehicles. As per its balance sheet, in 2017, Progressive had 13,087 $Millions of claims reserve.

For 2017, the "total insureds' money sitting on Progressive's bank account" was 8,904 $Millions + 13,087 $Millions = 21,990 $Millions.

We can find other items on the liability side of the balance sheet which are not linked to the policyholders' money: the "net deferred income taxes", the "dividends payable" and finally the "Accounts payable, accrued expenses, and other liabilities". We will group all these items in "other liabilities".

In 2017, the simplified view of the liabilities & shareholders' equity is therefore as follow:

1) Total insureds' money with Progressive: 21,990 $Millions
2) Total Debt: 3,306 $Millions
3) Total other liabilities: 3,616 $Millions
4) Shareholders' equity: 9,285 $Millions
5) Redeemable non-controlling interest: 504 $Millions

Total assets: 38,701 $Millions

We have now the following simplified balance sheet for 2017 and 2016:

ASSETS (in $Millions)	2017	2016
Assets without investment income	1,939	2,059
Investments producing an income	27,670	23,813
Insureds' cash not with the insurer	8,680	7,216
Other assets	413	340
Total assets	**38,701**	**33,428**

LIABILITIES & SHAREHOLDERS' EQUITY (in $Millions)	2017	2016
Insureds' money with Progressive	21,990	18,836
Debt	3,306	3,148
Other liabilities	3,616	3,002
Shareholders' equity	9,285	7,957
Redeemable non controlling interest	504	484
Total liabilities & Shareholders' equity and NCI	**38,701**	**33,428**

As Warren Buffet explained in 1996, "the Float is money that we hold that does not belong to us, it is like a deposit account with a bank". With our simplified view of the balance sheet, we can now estimate the float.

Float = "insureds' money with the insurer" – "insureds' cash not with the insurer"

Float in 2017 = 21,990 $Millions – 8,680 $Millions = 13,311 $Millions

In our example, why did we subtract the "uncollected insureds' cash" from the "money that the insurer has"?

There are several explanations for the previous subtraction. For instance, the premium for a policy could be paid after the effective date. When this happens, the "uncollected premium" is placed in an asset account called "premiums receivable" which appears on the balance sheet. But on the liability side, an "unearned premium" appears as well, thus the need to subtract the premium receivables from the UPR when looking for the float. We are describing on the next page the entries in the balance sheet with a simple example.

We assume a policy sold on the 1st of July 207, with the 1st of November 2017 as an effective date. The policy is for a 12-month cover, and the premium charged is $2,400. The premium is fully collected as cash on the 1st of January 2018. We are not considering the payment of commissions, taxes or expenses. From an accounting perspective, we will have the following entries in the balance sheet.

3rd Quarter 2017

Balance sheet at 30/09/2017

Assets		Liabilities	
Premium receivable	$0	Unearned premium	$0
Cash	$0		

4th Quarter 2017

Balance sheet at 31/12/2017

Assets		Liabilities	
Premium receivable	$2,400	Unearned premium	$2,000
Cash	$0		

1th Quarter 2018

Balance sheet at 31/03/2018

Assets		Liabilities	
Premium receivable	$0	Unearned premium	$1,400
Cash	$2,400		

In addition to the uncollected premium, we also need to consider the impact of the commissions paid upfront to the insurance distributors. The "deferred acquisition costs" which were described earlier, need to be subtracted from the UPR to come up with the float.

With our simplified view of Progressive's balance sheet, we can see the three sources of cash that the insurers are using to produce a decent investment income.

Progressive's sources of cash (in $Millions)	2017	2016
Float	13,311	11,621
Debt	3,306	3,148
Shareholders' equity	9,285	7,957
Total	**25,902**	**22,726**

After having reviewed Progressive's financial statement, we know that for its financial year 2017, the insurer was running an underwriting profit thus getting its "float" for free. We also know by now that it managed to increase its float and shareholders' equity while running a profit.

In the insurance market, it is well known that Glenn Renwick and his team have done an outstanding job to run Progressive Inc.

He retired in 2016 and got replaced by Tricia Griffith. As mentioned earlier in this book, it takes years to see the impact of a CEO on the performance of an insurer, therefore, at this stage we cannot assess her performance. By the end of 2017, Tricia Griffith seems to keep following the right path set by her predecessor. On the plus side, Tricia Griffith has spent her whole career within Progressive and climbed through the ranks, which is often a very good sign for investors.

For insurers, an increasing float is a healthy sign but is not sufficient, one needs to check the operation performance but also the origin of the float. As described with CBL insurance in a previous chapter, long tail businesses could bring some surprises and wipe out quickly a firm's capital if the pricing assumption or reserving approach is wrong.

Short and long tail businesses refer to the time it takes between the premiums are collected and the claims are paid out. Short tail businesses are for the products with claims which get paid out relatively fast (e.g. car insurance) and long tail businesses to those which last longer (e.g. builders' warranty products sold by CBL).

With "short tail" businesses, the insurers must invest the generated float in short-term securities (usually equity and debt securities) and/or other very liquid instruments (U.S. Treasuries, repo markets). These investments have relatively little risks and bring a small return for the insurers.

The long tail business allows the insurer to hold its investments over a longer period thus the opportunity to have a more diversified investment strategy but also gain higher returns. This is exactly what Berkshire Hathaway have been doing for years.

When looking at the performance of an insurer, one needs to also look at the investment income and the rate of return. How well does the insurer perform with its investments? But also, how aggressive are they with their investment strategy?

The float has made the fortune of Berkshire Hathaway which in the past has benefited from high yield investments. But as mentioned in our previous chapter, the insurers are currently going through a period with very low yields.

In our previous example, in 2017, we can see that Progressive gained a mere 2% on its total investments (see illustration 56 on the next page) whereas the inflation in the US for 2017 was 2.1%. This means that when we take into consideration the inflation, Progressive did not earn anything on its investments.

Clearly, Progressive's underwriting results are driving their earnings much more than the income from their investments. This is in line with the P&C industry. Long gone are the days when P&C insurers could deliver very high return on equity (ROE) while having a combined ratio above 100%.

With regards to Progressive, we can see that their products (Motor and/or household) are pushing them to invest in short-term securities which bring rather low returns.

Illustration 56: Progressive's return on investment

	2017	2016	2015
Total investments (in $Millions)	27,275	23,483	20,937
Investment income (in $Millions)	563	479	455
Investment expenses (in $Millions)	24	22	23
Return on investment	2.0%	1.9%	2.1%
Inflation in the US	2.1%	2.1%	0.7%

Having a low rate of return on investment does not mean that an insurer is performing poorly as we can see with Progressive which has been able to keep a rather low combined ratio for many years. Since its combined ratio was below 100%, Progressive was basically borrowing for free, money from its clients thus having a very interesting spread (see illustration 66 on the next page).

Illustration 66: Spread for Progressive's float

	2017	2016	2015
Combined Ratio	94.9%	96.6%	94.0%
Borrowing cost from customers	-5.1%	-3.4%	-6.0%
Investment rate of return	2.0%	1.9%	2.1%
Spread for Progressive's float	7.1%	5.3%	8.1%

It is worth comparing Progressive's performance with the one from the king of float: Warren Buffet and Berkshire Hathaway.

Berkshire Hathaway has been a leader in long-tail business for many years. They are specialized in jumbo reinsurance policies that leave them assuming long-tail losses already incurred by other property & casualty insurers.

****

What are the jumbo retro reinsurance businesses that Berkshire are managing?

As an example, we will explain the deal which was reached with AIG for the FY2017. In a statement, we learned that National Indemnity Company (NICO), agreed with American International Group (AIG) to acquire excess losses on old insurance policies via a retrospective reinsurance program (see the drawing on the next page).

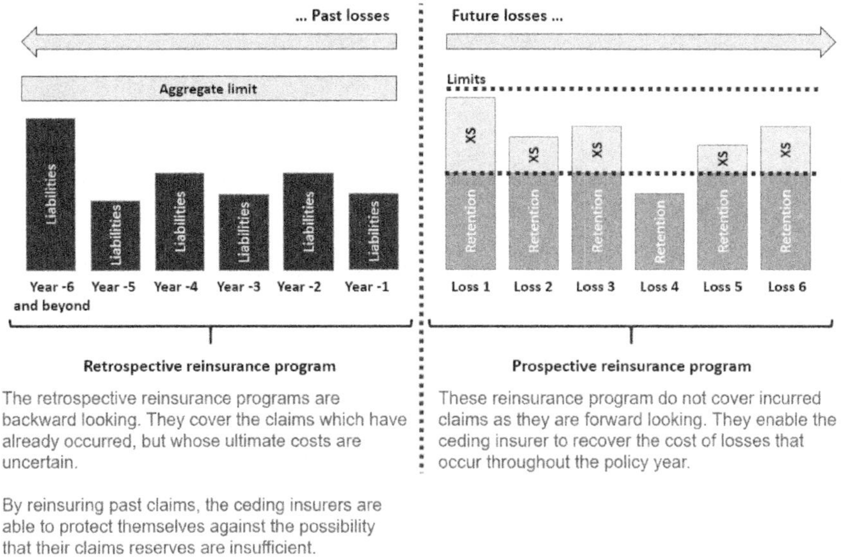

The agreement covers 80% of all of AIG's U.S. commercial long-tail exposures for accident years 2015 and prior. The premium paid by AIG was $9.8 billion paid in full by June 30, 2017.

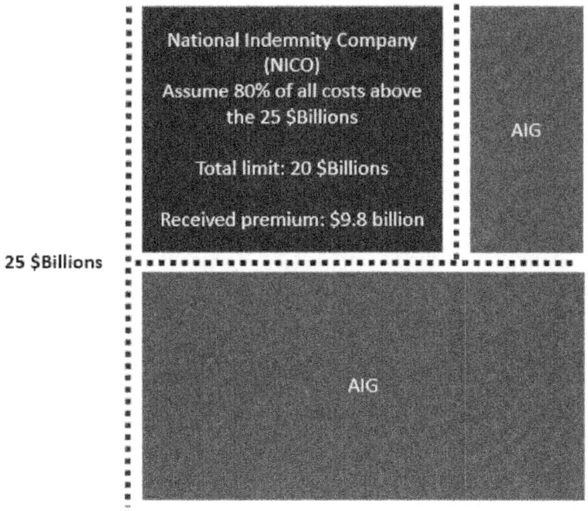

As part of the contract, NICO is assuming 80% of the net losses and net allocated loss adjustment expenses above the first $25 billion and NICO's overall limit of liability under the agreement is $20 billion, thus the word "jumbo" to describe such retrospective agreement.

****

From 1996 until 2017, Berkshire Hathaway's float has grown from 6.7 $Billion in 1996 to 114.5 $Billion in 2017. But we should exclude from our review the years prior to the Gen Re acquisition which took place in 1998 and the year 2017 which brought an abnormal growth (the one-off deal with AIG, which Buffett called the largest ever insurance policy in his letter to shareholders).
From 1998 until 2016, their float grew with an average annual rate of 8.2% per year.

Illustration 67: Berkshire's average float from 1996 - 2017

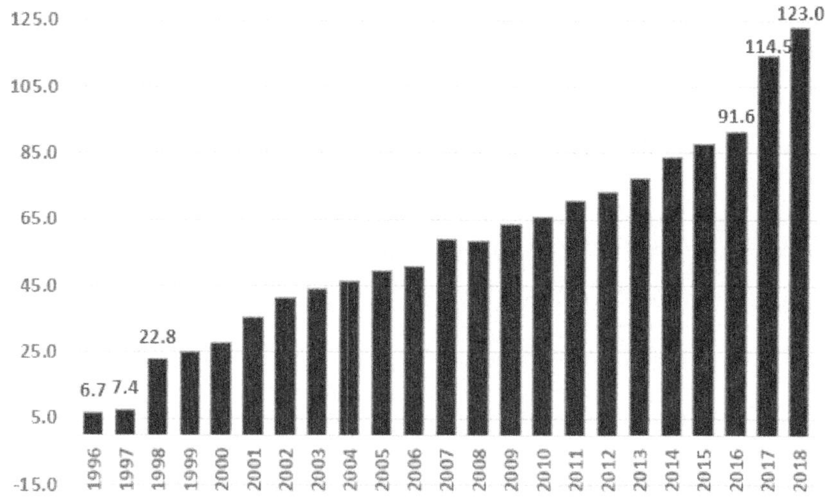

In 2017, a 14-year insurance win streak came to an end for Warren Buffet, with Berkshire posting an underwriting loss of roughly $3.2 billion and an average cost of 3% for its float (See illustration 68 on page 291)

Austin, Expert in finding lost Mojo

****

How did Warren Buffet come up with a cost of float of 3% for 2017?

As mentioned earlier, when an underwriting profit is achieved, the carrier is actually "paid" to hold other peoples' money. When there is an underwriting loss, the carrier is "paying" to hold their money. Since Berkshire Hathaway posted a pre-tax underwriting loss of 3.2 $billion with a total float of 114.5 $Billion, therefore, the cost of float was 2.8%.

$$Cost\ of\ Float = \frac{Underwriting\ Gain\ or\ loss}{Total\ Float}$$

$$2.8\% = \frac{3.2}{114.5}$$

****

Based on Berkshire's annual reports, we can see the years where an underwriting loss/gain took place and the cost of float with losses taking place in 1999, 2000, 2001, 2002 and 2017 (see the illustration 68 below).

Illustration 68: Berkshire's underwriting loss/gain and cost of float from 1996 – 2017 (in $Millions)

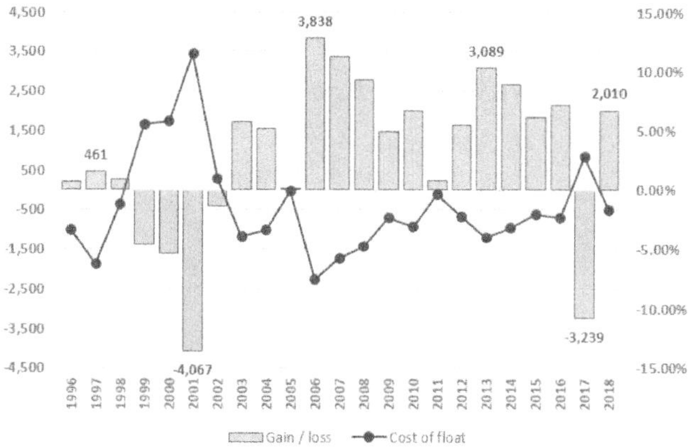

Posting an underwriting loss for the year does not necessarily result in having a loss for the year as the investment income could help.

In fact, since 1996, the insurance operations of Berkshire Hathaway have posted a yearly loss only once in 2001 because of the 09/11 terrorist attack, which was an extreme event (see the illustration 69 below). Excluding 2001, Berkshire had experienced additional underwriting losses which had always been covered by their investment income.

Illustration 69: Berkshire's UW loss/gain and investment income (in $Millions) from 1996 - 2017

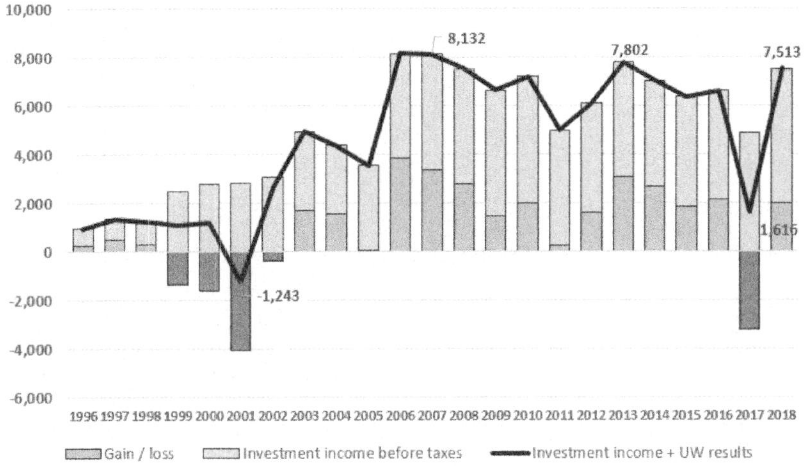

We can clearly see that the results of Berkshire's insurance operation are driven by their sizable float which delivers an impressive investment income. In any given year since 1997, Berkshire's investment income has been bigger than their underwriting results.

The David vs Goliath challenge: How did Progressive Corp perform when compared with Berkshire Hathaway?

Before jumping into the numbers, we need to point out that their business mix is very different to Berkshire's, mainly focusing on personal lines including motor insurance with the total collected premium being much smaller than Berkshire's (see illustration 70 below).

Illustration 70: Comparison Berkshire and Progressive for 2017 in $Millions

	Earned Premiums	Float
Berkshire	60,597	114,500
Progressive	25,730	13,311

In addition, the size of the float relative to the earned premiums is out of proportion for Berkshire when compared with Progressive. Again, the business mix explains this with Berkshire having very sizable long-tail insurance businesses (e.g. long-tail losses of other insurers) whereas Progressive focus on short-tail insurance businesses (e.g. repairs to cars are usually paid out within few days after a claim is filed).

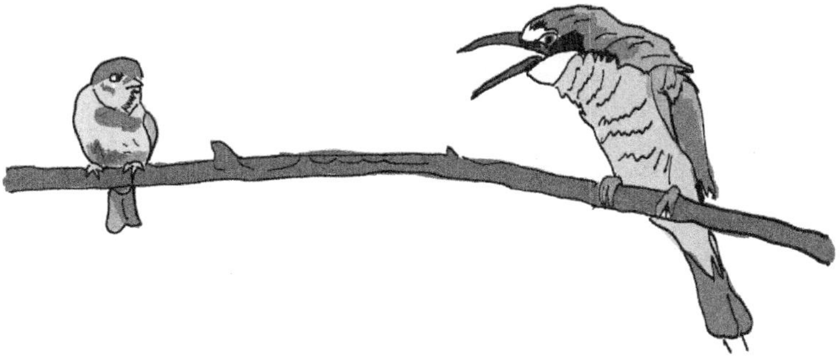

Since 1997, Progressive has experienced an underwriting loss only once in 2000 (see the illustration 71 below) which is better than Berkshire's performance: 5 years with an underwriting loss from 1997 to 2017. With their focus on long-tail, Berkshire is clearly managing "riskier" business than Progressive.

Illustration 71: Progressive's UW loss/gain and investment gains (in $Millions) from 1997 - 2017

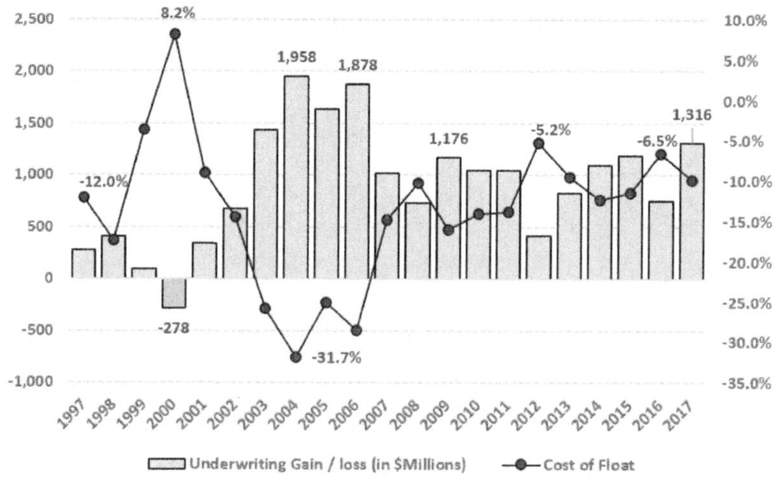

Progressive's investment income is the cherry on the cake which roughly adds 500 to 700 $Millions per year to their financial results. As for Berkshire, it covered their underwriting losses in 2000 (see the illustration 72 on the next page). But clearly, we can also see that their financial results are driven by their underwriting results instead of the gains from their investments. In other words, their business performance is not linked so much to the size of their float.

Illustration 72: Progressive's UW loss/gain and investment income (in $Millions) from 1997 - 2017

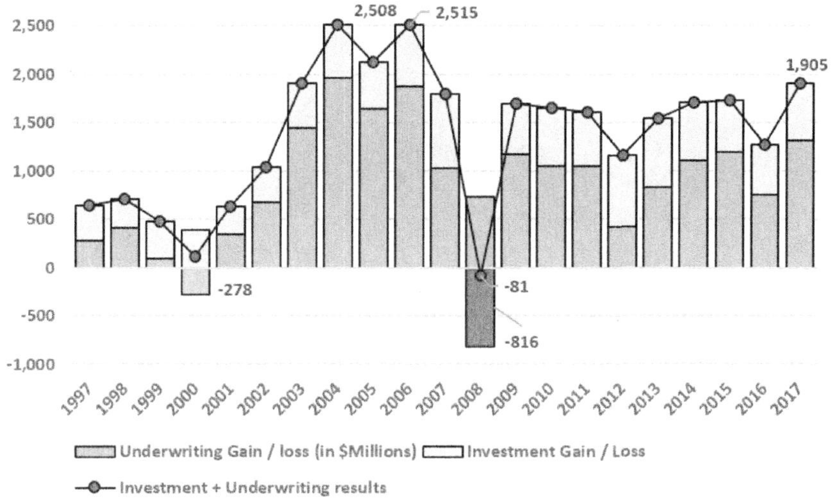

It is also worth mentioning that in 2008, their investment losses wiped out their underwriting gains thus a small loss of 81 $Millions for the whole year. Although Progressive had clearly followed a prudent investment policy for many years, unfortunately, they had some investments in other financial institution such as banks but also Fannie Mae and Freddie Mac, which was rather unfortunate.

When compared to Goliath, Progressive has had a rather impressive track record but how good is their financial performance against Berkshire?

We need to bring the two insurance players in a level playing field. To do so, we will divide their underwriting and investment results by their total earned premium (see the illustration 73 on the next page).

Illustration 73: Ratio of underwriting and investment results to earned premium for Progressive and Berkshire from 1996 - 2017

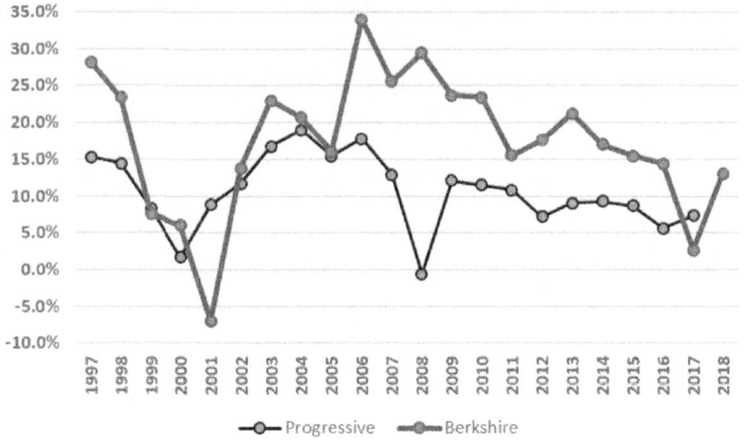

Over the years, we can see that Berkshire has outperformed Progressive except for 2001 and 2017.

Having said that, Berkshire's performance has been going down from its peak in 2006 while its float kept growing. This is also true for Progressive. We can easily link this decrease in their performance (relative to their earned premium) to the low-yield environment (see illustration 74 on the next page). For Berkshire, the increase of the competition for the jumbo reinsurance policies is also impacting the overall performance as it adds pressure to the reinsurance premium.

Based on our previous chapters, we all know that the interest rates are crucial in the way insurers are earning money: they are a key driver for the guarantees that life insurers offer to their clients; they impact the value of long-term liabilities but also the pricing of property and casualty insurance. Finally, they determine the returns that insurers make on their investments. Our match between David and Goliath clearly illustrates this.

Illustration 74: 10-year US treasury yield (2006 – 2018)

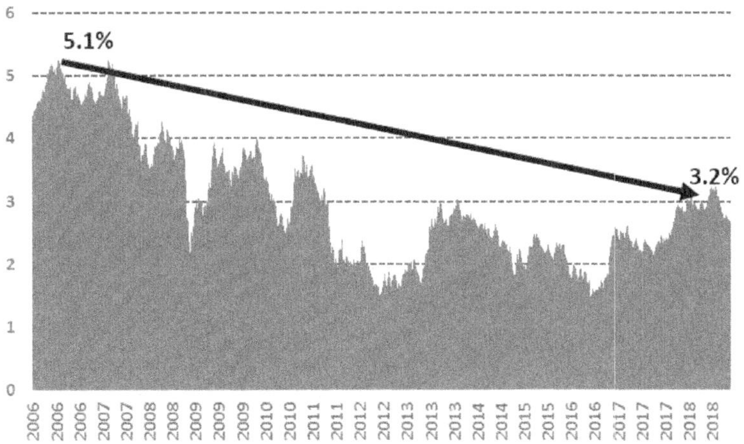

The allocation of investments for Berkshire is totally different than the one for Progressive and explains why they are generating a much higher investment income per earned premium than Progressive (See the illustration 75 on the next page).

Illustration 75: Progressive vs Berkshire investments

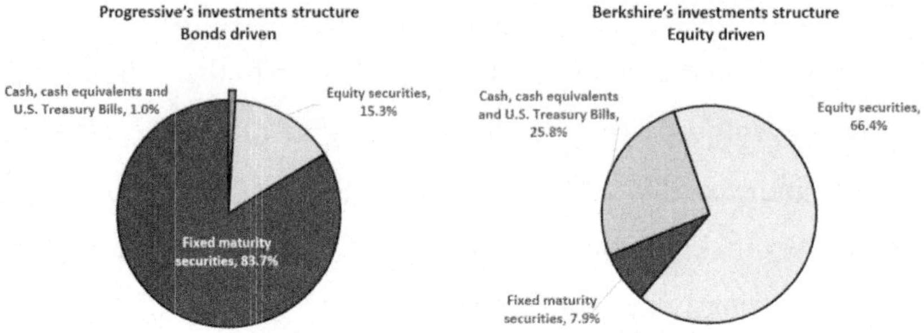

Berkshire's long-tail insurance business and the associated very large float allow them to embrace the risk-return trade-off. They can accept a higher possibility of losses thus rendering higher profits for their investments.

On the opposite, Progressive must follow a conservative approach with its investments since they are mainly managing short-term liabilities (with fast claims settlement) and cannot afford to lose money with their investments (see the 2008 event mentioned earlier in this chapter).

Illustration 76: Risk vs Reward pyramid and trade-off

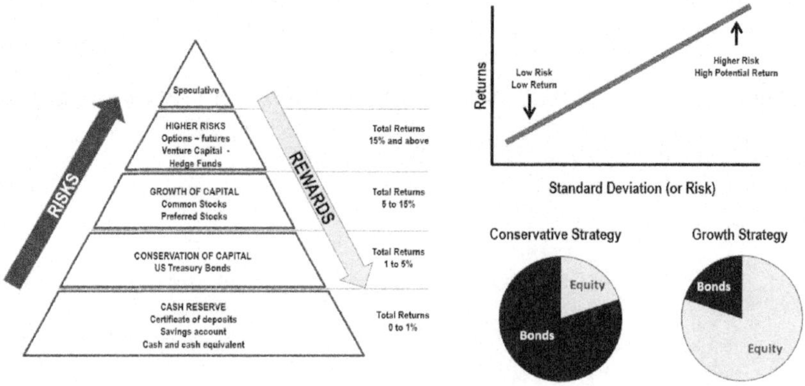

Although Progressive has been posting over the years an impressive track record in terms of profitability for their insurance business, they are not playing in the same league than Berkshire which can reach higher returns on their earned premiums. Berkshire's reinsurance arm brings the float which acts as the necessary steroids to boost the investment income for Berkshire insurance operations.

Illustration 77: Berkshire insurance operations

Berkshire insurance operation	Businesses	Premiums earned ($Millions)	Source of Float
GEICO	Personal lines	33,363	Low
Berkshire Hathaway Reinsurance Group	XS, QS, Retro, Annuity	15,944	High
Berkshire Hathaway Primary Group	Commercial lines	8,111	Medium

Progressive are effectively competing with Geico which are writing the same type of businesses. For instance, Geico is insuring 16 million cars in the US.

In this chapter, we went through what anyone should review when assessing the performance of an insurer. In addition, we went in length about the impacts of the float to the overall financial results.

We could have also covered the Return on Equity and/or Return on assets. For instance, in the current low yield environment, one would expect Insurers to have a ROE higher than 12%. The issue though with the ROE, is that the use of financial leverage could increase the return while the underlying operations are not having a good performance.

It is important to understand the mechanics of insurance to check if the financial results are stellar ... Finally, we have only looked at the performance backwards, but the future is also very important for any valuation and/or assessment.

We have all heard about how great Block Chain is and furthermore why Insurers are the dinosaurs which are threatened by the insurtech firms. One could also mention "digital disruption" as another buzzword. But what could be the future of the insurance industry? What could be the benefits of new technologies? And what are the challenges that they are facing? This is what we will see in the next chapter.

CHAPTER 11

THE DIGITAL CHALLENGES FOR THE INSURANCE INDUSTRY

When did the first automation take place in the insurance industry ?

What should insurers do to secure their future?

Are the Insurtechs changing the insurers' business model?

BY ERIC LEFEBVRE

Chapter Eleven

In a search for simplicity?

"Success is not final, failure is not fatal: it is the courage to continue that counts." — Winston S. Churchill

What is the most important thing for a financial institution? – Zurich, Spring 2018

Some consultants come to my office with questions about Insurance, how does it work? After some exchanges, I realised that for them it was all about "digital" and the use of analytics to offer the right products to the customers … How do we improve the customers' journey? Eric, the problem with the insurers is their legacy … they need to change their IT and be ready with digital platforms etc.

I must admit that I was really impressed with their use of all the right "buzzwords". As always, I enjoyed the exchange and challenged them back with a few questions.

First one being, why would a customer buy a life insurance cover online? What does she need to reach a decision? If you were to launch your digital offer, how will you attract your customers? Why would they come to you? What will differentiate your services from the competition?

There were few answers from them but quickly they showed their frustration as I did corner them in their logic which did not make sense at all to me ... They were talking about building their own digital ecosystem where the customers would buy their products ... I found the idea interesting but they did not answer my questions, nor did they have any clue on what will be offered to the clients.

I announced the end of the recess and offered to step back a bit before jumping into esoteric concepts.

I asked them a simple question: "What is the most important thing for a bank or even an insurer?"
Their eyes opened and they jumped into several things such as: (i) provide easy access to the customer's account online on a computer or a mobile phone, (ii) to get new customers thanks to a distinctive and unique experience.

I had a laugh and said: "No and no, these are not the most important things for a bank or an insurer. Of course, they will hopefully do everything to provide a good service for their customers but this is not the most important thing for them. To be honest, it seems that the marketing of the consulting firm is working very well with you, as you are repeating convincingly what most advisors are saying."

I changed my question to help them further: "Where are in Zurich the headquarters (HQ) of UBS, Credit Suisse, Zurich, Swiss Life, Swiss RE, etc.?" Of course, they knew exactly where these financial institutions were located.

"Have you seen their buildings? What do you think of them?"

I bet with them that if they were to go to Paris, London or even New York, the HQ for the banks and/or insurers will all be in very impressive buildings and prime locations. I told them that this is one of the most important things for financial institutions.

They still argued that in a digital world, no one cares about brick-and-mortar banks. “But why did the banks and/or insurers build those impressive buildings in the past?”
Then they almost got it, the consultants told me that it was to impress the customers. Frankly speaking, I had enough at that stage, I gave them the answer: “Brick-and-mortar is not the main thing, what the nice buildings brought in the past: trust! Banks and insurers are in the business of trust”.

The nice buildings and prime location were bringing confidence to the customers that their savings will be safe in the vaults of these institutions.

One of the main challenges for the financial institution is to gain and keep the trust of their clients: The trust that these institutions are solid from a solvency perspective and will be there for their clients when needed.

We shall keep this in mind when thinking about the future of insurance. “Digital Disruption” is one of many hypes which can be found everywhere and we will of course cover this as part of this chapter, but regardless of the innovation which will be brought to the market, trust will remain an essential aspect for insurance.

At this stage of the book, we all understand the mechanics of insurance (life and non-life) from pricing and/or selecting a risk, to managing a reserve and of course sometimes paying claims. All these activities have their own challenges, from selling a product to a new (or existing) customer to on-boarding her (capturing the necessary information) and finally at some point providing a service when she notifies the insurer of a claim.

To improve this whole process, the consultants will talk about the customer journey and the need to make it a unique experience. They have a point but we need to recognise that at the end of the day, it is all about data and furthermore how smoothly are the insurers able to interact with their customers.

Flood in North Carolina - possible challenges with insurers ...

So, what are the challenges in front of the insurers?

As we have seen earlier in this book, complexity is at the core of the insurance industry. From coming up with the right price to cover a risk or to manage the float, insurers must reliably manage and keep an important amount of information. They also need to provide an answer to their clients' problems and/or needs.

We can cover the possible challenges and potential solutions by looking at different areas:

- The insurance factory which manufactures and processes the products/solutions for the clients
- The distribution channels to engage with the customers/prospects
- The customers/prospects and their potential needs
- The shareholders who ultimately are supposed to agree with the insurers' strategy (allocation of the investments, etc.)

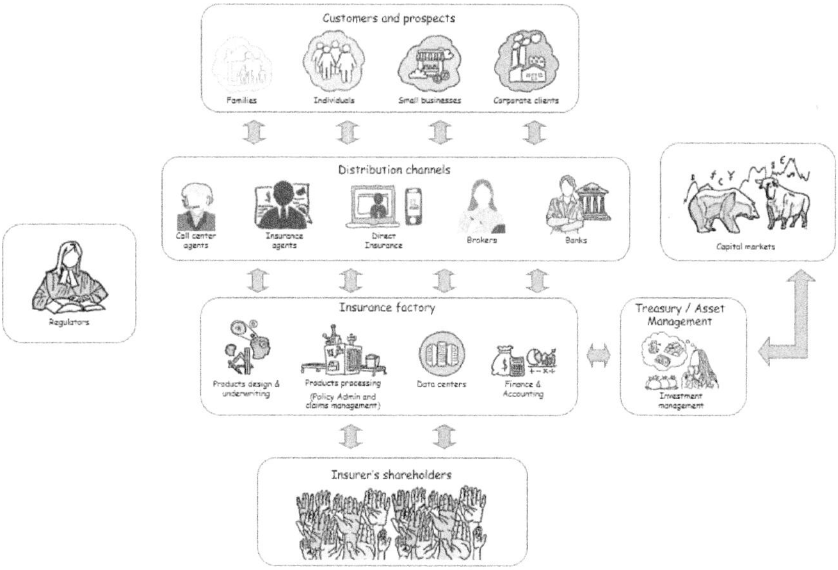

But all the different areas are somehow connected, for instance, a change to the customers' needs will affect the factory which will need to adapt its processes and machines.

Covering the insurers' challenges is like trying to untangle a skein of yarn, we need to start from somewhere and slowly go through all the loops.

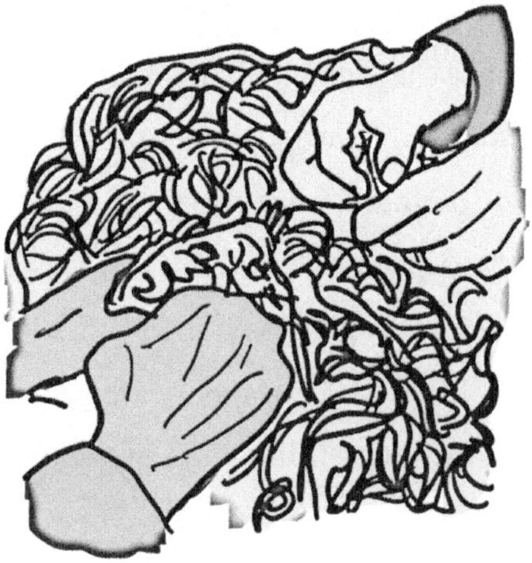

To untangle the key challenges, we will start with the product manufacturers and their challenges.

Lots of people are talking about the customers' needs and the services and/or products which are required to satisfy them but they tend to forget one aspect: how to manufacture these services or products? Could the factory do it with its existing tools and resources?

This could make us think of what Henry Ford said in 1906: "A customer can have a car painted any colour he wants as long as it's black".

To cover one of the "hottest topics" for the insurers, we will do some history and go back in time.

"Those that fail to learn from history, are doomed to repeat it." Winston Churchill

Surprisingly few people know this but Insurers (like bankers) are true "tech companies". They were the first one to embrace the new technology back in the 1950s and 1960s. They did not have a choice since, in the Western economies, people were buying cars "en masse" and insurers had to keep up with an important increase in demand for policies. The new technology was the perfect solution to manage reliably an ever-increasing amount of information.

It is interesting to notice that the insurers were just following the precepts which were detailed in Edmund C. Berkeley's book: "Giant brains; or, Machines that think" published in 1949!

The insurers understood that the computers could be used to maintain policy information in electronic files which would also be updated electronically going forward. There were clear benefits for servicing the clients and the opportunity to reallocate resources to activities with more added value.

For instance, before the adoption of the computers, Premium billing and accounting, which were (and still are) the easiest tasks in the insurance value chain, were very time-consuming. These tasks were requiring lots of clerical resources who would retrieve billing information from policy files, determine the amount of the premium due, type or produce policy notices on duplicating machines, and manually check the notices for errors.

Naturally, the insurers understood that these "low added-value" tasks were the ideal candidates for being "computerised".

They learned a lot when running these projects but were also very surprised: The tasks were much more difficult than originally anticipated and it took much more time to have the process managed by the computer than initially planned.

"Everything in war is very simple. But the simplest thing is difficult." - Carl von Clausewitz

The required efforts to analyse clerical work processes and develop the programs to simulate the recording, checking and decision-making processes of clerical workers revealed the hidden knowledge and skills of clerks and their supervisors.

In addition, when analysing the clerical routines, the teams discovered that the information needed to issue and monitor insurance policies were not standardized.

The resources were making decisions on a case-by-case basis, experiences and judgment were sometimes critical. There were multiple cases where the issuance of policies could not follow standard processes and procedures.

All these exceptions and surprises made it difficult to computerise some of the processes. To process the data with the available tools required that the processes and tasks were translated in very simple logic which could not handle ambiguities and/or exceptions. In other words, everything had to be specified and furthermore coded.

This should ring a bell to those of us who have been involved in implementing changes to existing processes within the insurance industry. Last century, the insurers went through dramatic changes to the ways that they had been processing information, they faced technical challenges but also human challenges.

"Theory must also consider the human element; it must accord a place to courage, to boldness, even to rashness"

The "computerise initiatives" had other consequences, the workload for the insurers' resources increased dramatically since the clerks, coders, and keypunch operators were needed to convert the existing records for use with computers. In today's world, we would see these activities as "data cleansing".

At the same time, the clients still had to be serviced with manual processes and tools. As a result, the insurers had to hire temporary clerks and additional keypunch operators to transfer name, address and retrieving information from the addressograph plates to punch cards.

In addition, the employees discovered that the information was not always accurate or of good quality thus having to contact the clients to correct wrong entries. These activities further added to the workload and increased the time to complete the tasks.

Finally, the insurers also discovered that they needed to gain the "buy-in" from their employees, to get them to share their knowledge of the "unwritten" procedures.

To achieve this, they communicated on the opportunities brought by computers such as performing more rewarding and demanding tasks. With the help of the computer manufacturers, they also created internal learning schools to train their employees on the new technology. These employees were to maintain the programmes going forward.

By the early 1960s, the main applications were dealing with unearned premium, premium accounting, sales statistics (commissions and sales) but also premium billing which was an input to reserving. And by the end of the 1960s, the processing of claims, the issuance of policies and other accounting activities were also computerised.

Key lessons from these projects

In the 1950s and 1960s, it took much more time than anticipated for the insurers to "computerise" their processes. The lack of documentation on their processes and furthermore the management of exceptions brought additional complexity. Finally, to secure the success of their transformation, the insurers discovered that their employees were their true assets and their knowledge was invaluable.

Over the following decades, the insurers kept investing in their systems to improve their performance and the services delivered to the customers. They also changed the technology when required.

But in the 1980s and 1990s, some of these investments were reduced and the approach with technology changed. There are several reasons for this including cost-cutting initiatives which took place because of the 1989 financial crisis.

The consolidation which took place in the 1990s did not help either. Some of these mergers were successfully managed (the Axa Story) and others ended with tears. Most of the mergers did not deliver the expected benefits fast enough and as a result, the insurers had to stop the rationalisation of their portfolios and furthermore moving their policies towards single platforms, thus missing the opportunity to simplify their IT architectures.

By the year 2010, many insurers were still running their policies on multiple old platforms. Some of these platforms were put in place back in the 1970s. We have all heard stories of Insurance IT departments buying old servers from eBay to gather parts for maintaining their infrastructure.

And it does not come as a surprise to meet in an IT department, “retirees” who are employed as contractors to maintain these ageing systems.

On the factory side, the main challenges for the insurers are linked to their legacy and history. The mergers which took place in the 1990s and 2000s enabled some of them to become very big in terms of assets under management and volume of policies/customers. But because of these transactions, there are running multiple production lines with often ageing technologies and ever-increasing costs to maintain them.

These systems are often managing very old policies, especially for the life insurance products. When an insurer must move its portfolios to a new platform, they sometimes encounter some surprises. For instance, I experienced myself the case of a process running overnight for a life insurance product which only had one in-force policy. When we investigated the case, we discovered that the policyholder was long deceased!

In 2018, the regulators in the US estimated that more than $2 billion in benefits have gone unclaimed from lost or forgotten life insurance policies.

InsuR running overnight batches to update the value of Maria's life insurance policy

Maria forgot to mention the existence of her life insurance policy to her heirs ...

What are the problems with these legacy systems?

The insurers' legacy systems are like the Ford T example which was used to start this part of the book. The systems have been stable and reliable over their lifetime but unfortunately are not able to adapt to the new technology trends such as mobile, social or Internet of things.

Furthermore, the business side of the organisation is often complaining of the required time in months or years to put to market new products. In addition, the maintenance costs and change costs for complying with new regulation are getting onerous.

Finally, in the case of the legacy systems, the last straw that breaks the camel's back is the age of the people who put in place the systems and are maintaining them. They are often "baby boomers" who are reaching retirement age as stated earlier in this chapter.

In recent years, these challenges have pushed most of the insurers to revamp their IT platforms by either buying off-the-shelf solutions or building their own platforms. The tasks are often Dantean as the insurers must replace systems which are the results of several decades of adjustment and development which in most cases have been badly documented.

In addition, to be able to deliver the required services for the customers, these systems are sharing information with each other through interfaces which also need to be replaced.

We are often referring to these projects as the "spaghetti plate" challenge, since the blueprint of an IT architecture often looks like it.

The spaghettis are representing the interfaces and the platforms or applications being the meat in a Bolognese plate. In other words, replacing these systems is often a mess as people are opening a Pandora box.

How to effectively manage or reduce the complexity of these projects?

The budgets allocated to change an IT platform fluctuate a lot ranging from a few million dollars to hundreds of million dollars. The insurers are somehow "rediscovering" what their predecessors went through in the 1950s with unexpected complexities and furthermore undocumented processes.

One of the main issues being that they are somehow not simplifying their products nor activities. For instance, some of the insurers are copying their products from one old system to a new one without an attempt to simplify them, this is especially true for the life insurance industry.

Furthermore, they opt for undergoing a massive change to their IT systems with an unknown outcome instead of going to an incremental change approach. Thus, running the risk that by the time their changes are fully implemented, the solution in place might already be totally outdated and their customers not interested with the "new products" being offered.

You can't just ask customers what they want and then try to give that to them. By the time you get it built, they'll want something new.

Steve Jobs

To embrace change, the insurers should follow the approach advised by Professor Vijay Govindarajan in his great book the "three box solutions". The fundamental idea behind his solution, is that the future is now and not what a firm has to do in the future. In other words, if an insurer wants to remain and/or be a leader in 2025, the required activity does not start in 2025 but start today.

As per Vijay Govindarajan, an insurer (any corporation) needs to take actions in three boxes:

1) Box one is to manage the present. In this box, the insurer will have to improve the efficiency of its current businesses.
2) Box two is about the past. This represents the activities and/or mindset from the past which need to be abandoned.
3) Box three is about creating the future.

Box one brings the necessary income for today and furthermore the investments to finance the future (Box three). While achieving this, the insurer will have to leave the "old world" and/or "habits". Box two is really about that, the insurer needs to stop selling the products which are not fit for the future and may also need to sell old portfolios.

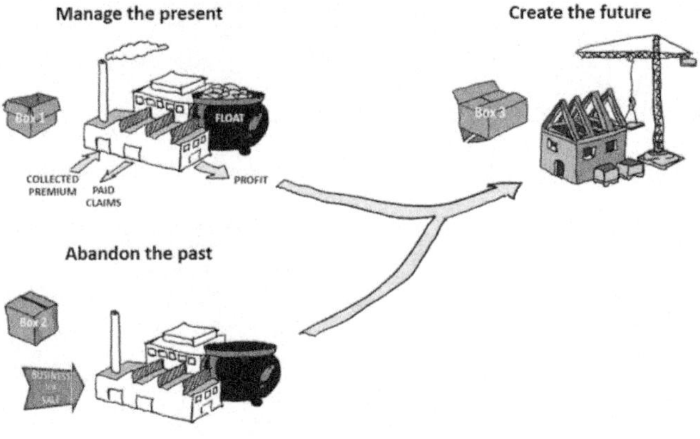

We will use an example to illustrate how to use this concept before running a massive IT change.

****

Example 12: IT Changes with InsuR Germany

Let's assume that InsuR Germany is running several insurance platforms from the 1980s and the early 1990s. They see that their budgets for regulatory changes are going up on a yearly basis but also the time to implement these changes.

Their business people are also joking about the time it takes to get a new product running in their system, "At the pace, you are delivering our projects, we won't sell these products until the cows come home."

In addition, most of the IT resources who are running these systems, are late in their fifties and will soon retire thus further jeopardising the future of these platforms.

The management decides that it is time to "revamp" the IT infrastructure and landscape. The first estimates are very high with a total budget exceeding the 200 €Millions.

When looking at this figure, one should wonder how many policies must be sold or managed to pay for this.

The InsuR management knows that they must invest in their "machines" in order to grow their business and/or continues to service their existing customers in Germany but such budget seems out of proportion to their income.

Before starting any changes to their IT platforms, the management decides to follow Vijay Govindarajan's approach and to review their current products and services. Their goals are (i) to identify the services and/or products which do not represent Insur's future (the box 2), (ii) clearly state what could be the future for InsuR (the box 3) and (iii) properly manage their current "gold mine" which would require some investments to extend its "lifetime".

With the current low investment yields and higher capital requirements for Solvency II, InsuR Germany decides to put in "run-off" the portfolios of life insurance policies which offer a guaranteed rate of return. These portfolios will be part of Box 2. The IT investments will be kept to a minimum while InsuR discusses with private equity funds which are willing to purchase such portfolios.

The capital light investment products (described in a previous chapter) will be part of box 1 as they represent what the insured want today. This will also include the opportunity for clients to invest in ESG (environmental, social and governance) funds. The non-life products such as Motor, Household coverages are kept in box 1. The investments in new platforms will be used as an opportunity to simplify the products and push for additional services to the clients as a competitive differentiator. The management also requests to have a quick and measurable return on investment for any changes to the IT platforms including setting-up new ones.

As part of box 1, the management will push the organisation to be more focused and to follow a surgical approach to avoid large, multi-year projects. Instead, the employees will have to work on shorter, sprint-like programs that deliver new capabilities every few months.

InsuR Germany will follow a simplification initiative which will focus on adding value to the customers (internal or external). The incremental changes to the processes will not apply to everything. The teams will assess which part of their processes and services offered need to be excellent and which one could have inferior performance.

In terms of culture, InsuR Germany will ensure that their teams and people do not seek the Rolls Royce version of a product when a Chevy (or Passat) is all that is needed. Their choices will be heavily informed by the needs of customers.

Box 3 is about the future. Of course, it is very difficult to predict what the customers will ask in 10 to 20 years from now but an organisation can prepare itself for it. In the case of InsuR, the management decides to consider their customers' life cycle and to build a value proposition for every step of their life.

The use of new technologies and tools will be considered to better serve the "silver economy" (the generation of the baby boomers) but also the younger generation such as the millennials and/or the generation Z. As part of the box 3, InsuR will explore the new services which need to be put in place for their clients.

The management also understands that this is not so much about implementing new technologies but rather becoming more "agile" in order to be able to adapt to the new changes which will come.

The box 3 is therefore also about changing the culture and the organisation to follow the precepts of Leon C. Megginson:
"According to Darwin's Origin of Species, it is not the most intellectual of the species that survives; it is not the strongest that survives, but the species that survives is the one that is able best to adapt and adjust to the changing environment in which it finds itself".

****

Before even considering changing their IT platform and/or modernising their legacy platforms, the Insurance organisation should focus on reviewing their product lines: which offerings should be kept and which one should be discontinued without regrets?

Are there insurers which are currently following Vijay Govindarajan's approach?

We cannot find such information but we can observe what Axa are doing under the management of their visionary CEO, Thomas Buberl and categorise their transformation activities within the "3 boxes" framework.

Thomas Buberl presents his 2020 strategy as follow:
"Focus, the first pillar of our strategy, is about taking actions today to ensure we deliver what our stakeholders expect from us. [...] At the same time, the second pillar is to transform our company to ensure tomorrow's growth".

In addition, to this Axa announced that they will focus on growing their profitable Protection & Health business both while tackling the Savings challenge by promoting hybrid and capital light products.

For their Property&Casualty business, they also mentioned their ambition to actively grow their commercial lines footprint.
Axa put their words into actions and, in 2016 sold their UK investment and pensions business to Phoenix Group, exiting a mature life assurance market and focusing on faster-growing emerging economies. This could be a "box 2" activity.

In addition, in 2018, Axa Group partially listed its US life insurer, Equitable.
For Axa's parent company, the Equitable deal provided a way to unlock capital. The proceeds from listing about 20% of Axa Equitable Holdings helped the French insurer fund its biggest-ever acquisition: a $15.3 billion takeover of XL Group Ltd.

The bold manoeuvre was to help Axa shift toward property and casualty insurance while reducing its exposure to savings activities in the U.S. We can clearly categorise these events as typical "box 2" initiatives. Furthermore, the IPO proceeds in the US, is also used to finance a "box 3" initiative which is the acquisition of XL Group.

As mentioned in our InsuR example, to survive, any organisation needs to be "agile" enough to embrace a change. In 2017, Axa simplified and decentralized its organization, removing two layers of management to facilitate local decision-making. In other words, as part of box 1, Axa is currently optimising their processes and organisation.

Axa is not the only insurer which has decided to transform its operations and become leaner.

When taking over Zurich Insurance in 2016 following some bad results in 2015 (see previous chapter 3), Mario Greco confronted the reality head-on and faced the facts about the state of its organisation and business and then worked with his team to bring the firm to a better place.

Zurich Insurance decided to remove some management layers by combining the management of its life and non-life businesses but also simplifying its regional structures. In a statement, Mario Greco announced, "This new organisation and strong accountability, empowerment and outcome orientation will be the foundation for our future strategy ... we will see greater market focus and simplification, and deliver the transformation we need for future success in a disciplined way."

In addition, we can also see that Zurich is pursuing a growth strategy around travel insurance. In 2017, they bought the travel insurance platform Cover-More. In 2018, they accelerated the growth of their Cover-More business with the acquisition in Latin America of additional travel capabilities, thus becoming a truly global travel insurer. We can assume that Zurich is betting on travel insurance which offers capital-light products with low volatility. We could see these acquisitions as part of their box 3.

Why are the insurers getting leaner and/or simplifying their organisation?

Of course, the low-yield environment (on the investment side) is forcing the insurers to make major changes to their business models and furthermore to reduce costs. As we have seen in our previous chapters, the interest rates have a big impact on the pricing of insurance products (life insurance, long-term liabilities, P&C). To keep their customers or gain new ones, the insurers cannot increase too much their premium, therefore they must do what they were doing in the past for less …

New incumbents are also set to disrupt the $5 trillion insurance market. While having to recognise these new incumbents, traditional insurers are finding it difficult to adapt their models to clients with changing expectations. As mentioned earlier, the organisations which will survive are those which are able to adapt.

Some of the international insurers with their legacy and size could be seen like a fleet of old ocean supertankers that will have difficulty turning around in a short time or stop.

The issue is that these supertankers must compete with small and very mobile vessels.

On the plus side, the small vessels do not have the financial power of the big insurers. Although some of the insurers are not fully fit to go through the current stormy waters, they are still strong enough to stay afloat while "reinventing" themselves. They have lots of funds which could be invested to "reinvent" themselves.

As per Michael Porter's definition, "Operational efficiency means you are running the same race faster, but strategy is choosing to run a different race because it is the one you have set yourself up to win". It is, of course, good to work on "box 1" but as the Allianz CEO Oliver Bäte said in 2006, cost-cutting "is not a strategy". As seen with Axa, Insurers do have to come up with a strategy for their future.

What is the bigger picture, why are the insurers shifting towards health or protection products? Why are all insurers talking about embracing the digital wave?

Let's face it, we are in front of rapid changes to our world with people showing their fears. The emergence of the iPhone which revolutionised the mobile phone industry in 2007 is just the tip of the iceberg. The 2007 - 2008 financial crisis is probably much more interesting from a change perspective, as it represents the end of a business cycle.

A similar situation took place after the 1929 crash with the surge of destructive forces which led to a terrible outcome. At that time, the world was in a transitional period between two major business cycles, and most likely the same is true today.

Like the tectonic plates, two major business cycles or "macro waves" are currently colliding thus having distortion taking place economically and socially.

Drop, cover and hold on to
withstand the quake

****

What is a Business Cycle?

A business cycle is the natural rise and fall of economic growth that occurs over time. Each business cycle has four phases. These phases are (i) expansion, (ii) peak, (ii) contraction and (iv) trough. These phases don't occur at regular interval but have recognizable indicators.

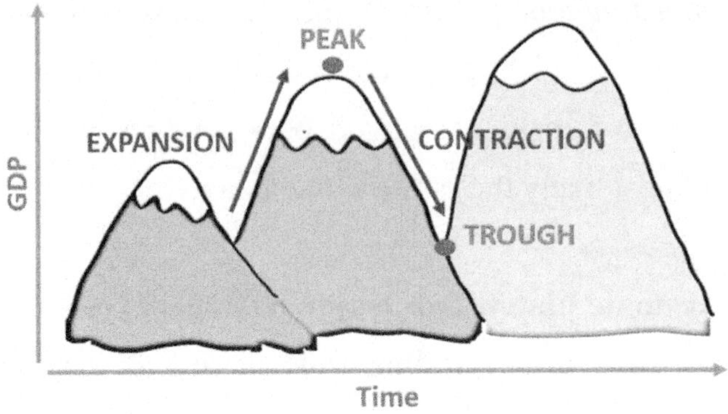

The Expansion phase takes place between the "through" and the "peak". In the contraction phase, the GDP growth falls below 2% and when it turns negative, we have a recession. The Stock market enters a bear market as investors sell.

****

Before describing the two macro waves, we will introduce the Kondratieff theory which was formulated by the Soviet economist Nikolai Kondratieff at the beginning of the 20th century.

chapte

According to Kondratieff, economies follow the path of long-term dynamic cycles or waves. A long wave lasts for 40–60 years, and consists of a period of rapid economic growth, followed by stagnation or depression (see the illustration 69 on the next page).

Illustration 69: Crises – The Power of Creative Destruction Rolling 10-year returns on the S&P 500 since 1814

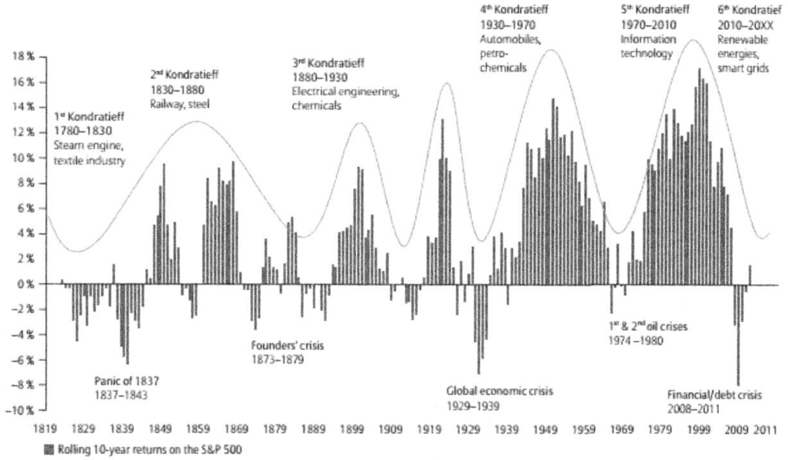

Source: Robert J. Shiller, Stock Market Data used in "Irrational Exuberance" Princeton University Press, 2005, Datastream; Allianz GI Capital Market Analysis.

Some research and many economic indicators tend to support the interpretation that, since the economic crisis of 2008, we now find ourselves in the last stages of the 5th wave and are about to enter the 6th wave.

This transition period between the 5th wave and the 6th wave could explain the stock tsunami ("reset") which will take place in the coming years but also the big technology changes which are happening. According to the theory, each wave is defined by a specific set of technologies and societal practices that are unique to that wave.

One could assume that the 6th wave will address some of the below aspects:

- Demographic changes with an ageing population and need to ensure longevity
- The growth of health services
- Increase of environmental concerns and the needs for resource efficient technologies
- Potentially moving away from fossil fuels (new sources of energy)
- The dominance of artificial intelligence and the rise of robots

Before jumping into conclusions, it is worth checking the world demographics. In the 20th century, the world population grew from 1.6 billion to 6.1 billion while the average life expectancy of a European grew from 40 years to over 60 years. The 21st century will be a century of an ageing population. By the end of this century, the average proportion of people over 60 will rise from the current 10% or so to somewhere between 25–45%.

This represents a huge disruption to the economy and society. It is also likely that the world will see the end of population growth. Europe, North America and East-Asia, will see a rapid ageing and a declining fertility rate.

Although tackling the future energy problem will be an important challenge for the next Kondratieff wave, we can assume that the sixth wave will also be a health-related cycle. It will be about healing people and furthermore make it possible for them to live much longer than today.

Finally, we also know from history that the transitional period between two Kondratieff waves facilitates the entry of new types of innovations (see the illustration 69). We are currently talking about self-driving cars which would reduce the risks of accidents thus potentially making motor insurance all but irrelevant. The rise of artificial intelligence and robots will also bring challenges and opportunities.

The insurers like any other institutions are currently navigating through the transition period and positioning themselves for the future. This could explain why Axa chose to expand its offerings in health but also commercial insurance.

What about the digital revolution which is to change the industry forever?

With regards to the digital wave, we need to ask ourselves a basic question – What is the first thing we do in the morning when we wake up?

We can bet that a lot of us are using our mobile phone as an alarm clock and as a result check social media. The statistics are telling us that 2 out of 3 people check their phones within 5 minutes of waking up!

The average American spends more than 3 hours on a smartphone per day, and most usage is dedicated to messaging and social media, as well as navigation. A decade ago, the average person spent approximately 90 minutes a day using their phone for a different purpose.

The insurers are developing apps which can be used to buy and/or check the status of our insurance policies. But this is already the "present" and does not represent the future, of course, some insurers are late with having a presence in that space.

What is interesting about the "digital wave" is the opportunity for insurers and other firms to collect information about consumer behaviour. This information could provide an edge to some insurers as they could provide a very precise price of the covered risk and/or design new products to protect their customers.

The artificial intelligence could be used to improve the insurers' risk management e.g. a real-time forward-looking solvency which would use publicly available information. Machine learning could also benefit pricing as we saw with Axa in Japan, which used machine learning in a Proof of Concept to optimize pricing by predicting "large-loss" traffic accidents with 78% accuracy.

There are plenty of opportunities and challenges with the digital wave, we can find several books or articles about these but one thing does not change which is at the core of the insurance business model: “the pooling of risks”. As described in the very first chapter of this book, our ancestors already understood the benefits of putting together some of their savings in a large pool of funds to protect each other.

We should not talk about “digital” but rather “technology” as it is clearly about that. The rapid evolution of technology is providing opportunities for the industry to improve its services to the customers.

Are we seeing new business models for insurance?

A few years ago, we heard about a new concept called “peer to peer insurance”. Many people showed some excitements about this concept which was “revolutionising” insurance. The reality though is that these players are just going back to the fundamental definition of insurance: “the mutualisation of losses”.

Peer-to-peer insurance is a form of risk sharing where small groups of people gather through apps or online. In 2010, Friendsurance developed this concept, which rewards small groups of users with a cash-back bonus at the end of each year if they remain claimless.

They came up with this idea as they thought that traditional insurance products are rather expensive and lack transparency: people pay high premiums each year and get nothing in return. As we saw in our previous chapters, we cannot disagree with this statement but we also need to recognise that the insurers are paying claims.

In 2016, Lemonade, a poster child of the insurtech movement, went even further with their statements: "Knowing that every dollar denied to you in claims is a dollar more to your insurer, brings out the worst in us all … we architected Lemonade to avoid conflicts of interest. We take a flat 20% fee and give unclaimed money to causes our policyholders care about. Since we don't pocket unclaimed money, we can be trusted to pay claims fast and hassle-free."

One should admit that this sounds great but by now, after having read this book, we are able to see that the 20% flat fee is not that spectacular. In chapter 10 of this book, we saw that "Progressive" a traditional insurer is running a 21.6% expense ratio which is not so far from Lemonade's fees. There is a big catch though, in the case of "Progressive", the 21.6% are covering the commissions paid to the distributors and the costs of running the insurance operations. With regards to "Lemonade", there are no commissions to be paid to an agent and/or broker since the products are distributed directly.

It is worth mentioning that often the "traditional insurers" are charging the same price for an insurance product sold directly via their website or via an agent, even if a commission is paid to the agent. One would expect that the products sold directly would be cheaper.

In a great article "Don't Believe the Hype – The Lemonade Story", Nick Lamparelli went further in describing what it is all about: "Lemonade is a broker by another name. Another of Lemonade's selling points is that insurers have a conflict of interest in that they make money by denying claims."

Nick Lamparelli took the time to further detail the organisation and show that, Lemonade is two organisations: A broker which gets 20% of the premium and an insurance firm which uses 80% of the premium for paying claims. The interesting part though is that they can use the full power of AI and robotics to accelerate the issuance of a policy and claims processing. The organisation does not have the legacy of traditional insurers thus the ability to be rather fast and furthermore to displace "nice apps and website" (not to mention nice videos on YouTube).

There are of course plenty of opportunities to improve the insurance industry and change some of its practices. We saw in earlier chapters that the insurers should be much more transparent with their business models, especially for life insurance. By now, with this book, we should have understood the mechanics of insurance and how it works. We can see insurers as organisation which manage "pools of money" on behalf of a community of insureds (their customers) and therefore charge a fee for this.

With regards to "disrupting the insurance industry", wearing a tee-shirt (or a black turtleneck) in front of media or investors, does not make the CEO of an Insurtech company a Steve Jobs. In another industry, we saw the possible results of this with Theranos and its founder Elizabeth Holmes.

But we must admit that fresh ideas which could "shake" the industry, are welcome and Lemonade has been clearly successful with this.

What is the next thing for insurers?

Let's face it, most of us (if not all of us) are bad at predicting the future. At the height of the internet bubble, lots of ideas were flying around but only a few if any predicted the success of google or amazon. Who would have thought then that because of Amazon, the retail market would go through dramatic changes? No one either had anticipated the impact of social Media to the younger generations: the millennials and the generation Z.

We would all agree that it is very difficult to anticipate what will happen. Having said that, we all know that insurers (like any other firms) must identify and be ready for any changes on their horizons.

In his great book, "Market-Led Strategic Change", Nigel F. Piercy provided the competitive box (see below) to illustrate that in most markets, there are things which can destroy the incumbents if they have a tunnel vision.

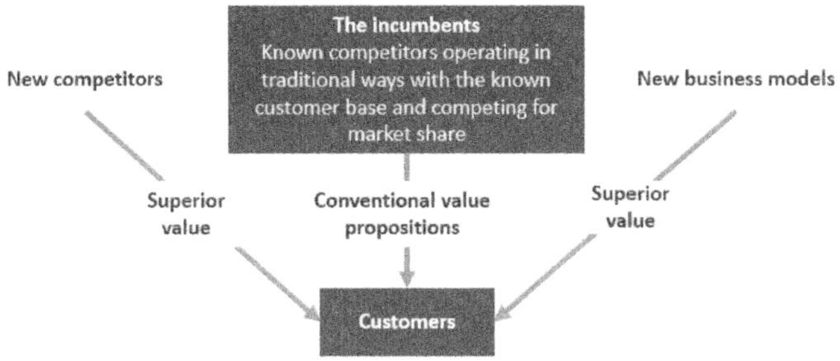

There is an endless list of corporations which have disappeared because of new competition and/or a technological change, to name a few: Kodak, Polaroid, Compaq, Barnes & Noble, etc. These firms had a tunnel vision and tried to improve their own technologies and/or services instead of changing their business models to address their clients' needs.

In his book, Nigel F. Piercy also described an approach: "revolution, reinvention and renewal" which could be used to build an understanding of the realities of market-led strategic change in companies (see below)

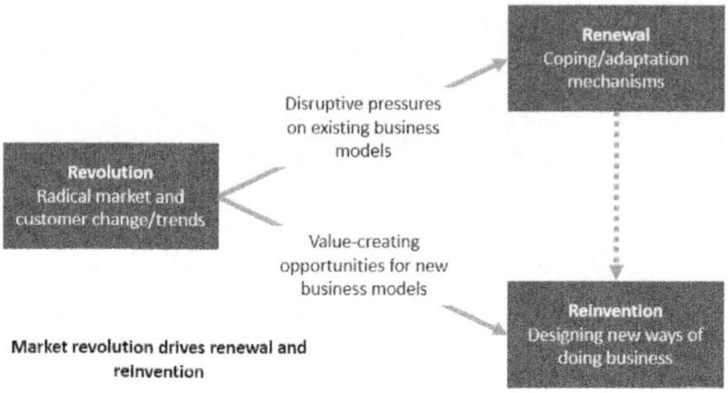

Contrary to popular belief, Lemonade or Friendsurance have not created a new business model for insurance. Like the Romans (see chapter 1), they are pooling their customers' premiums to cover future claims. But they have simplified the products and made the purchase of insurance easy for individuals.

In the US, CoverWallet has been shaking the insurance market for small businesses with a simplified onboarding process. As a result, Berkshire Hathaway followed suit and launched in 2019 a simplified product dedicated for the SMEs called "three" (sold directly without brokers).

We can consider that in most markets, the customers want simplified and easy to understand products. This is the revolution which is currently happening for insurance. The challenge for the incumbents is not the products but the technology which enables such simplification, they must review their pricing approach and furthermore their "factories" (described earlier in this chapter).

InsuR missed the millennials and the generation Z.
They have decided to be ready for the alpha

Finally, for years, motor insurance has been the cash cow for most insurers globally. All "experts" (or self-declared experts) are predicting the end of motor insurance with the adoption of driverless cars.

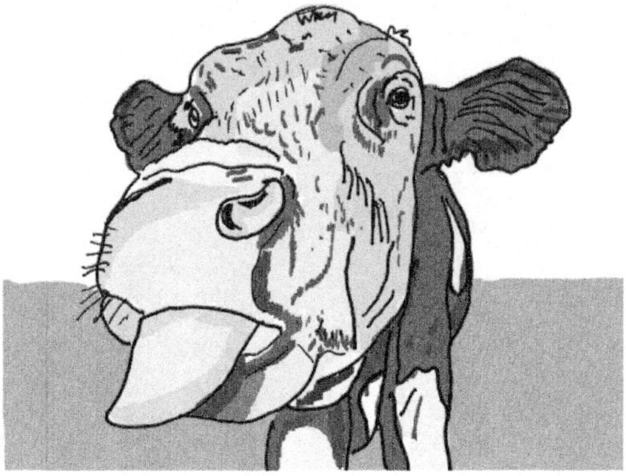

Having gone through the dot-com bubble, we can assume that people tend to overestimate the speed of change (adoption rate) and underestimate the potential impacts (see our previous discussion on the tunnel vision). There is no doubt that the motor insurance market will change dramatically when the fleet of driverless cars will be big enough, the key question is: when will this tipping point take place?

When this event occurs, the insurance industry will have to find new sources of income. We may assume that the insurers will shift to new services or products while people are adopting driverless cars.

The tipping point is probably decades away since cars last about 10 years. If we assume that fully driverless cars hit the market, en masse by 2025 and that people are only buying driverless cars when switching their vehicles, we can estimate that by 2035, 50% of the fleet will have such vehicles. We might have a full fleet of driverless vehicle by 2045. The legislation in the countries may push for having a higher adoption rate over the years thus accelerating the process.

In a "driverless" future, the liability will most likely shift from the drivers to the manufacturers. In this new reality, we could wonder if the manufacturers will buy a product liability cover from the traditional insurers. They could choose to manage their own pool of money to pay for the claims which will occur, as they will have the necessary data to effectively assess any claims.

The insurers will have to find other risks which could provide the same level of income, those who won't be able to shift to new sources of income will most likely disappear.

"There is one thing stronger than all the armies in the world, and that is an idea whose time has come" - Victor Hugo

About the Author

Thank you for reading! Please add a short review on Amazon and let me know what you thought!

Printed in Great Britain
by Amazon

56408694R00205